SEXUAL

A Program for Positive Change

HARASSMENT AND TEENS

- ► Case Studies
- ► Activities
- ► Questionnaires
- ► Laws
- ► Guidelines
- ► Policies
- ► Procedures
- ► Resources
- ► And More

Susan Strauss

with Pamela Espeland

Free Spirit®
PUBLISHING

Library of Congress Cataloging-in-Publication Data
Strauss, Susan
    Sexual harassment and teens : a program for positive change ; case studies, activities, questionnaires, laws, guidelines, policies, procedures, resources, and more / Susan Strauss with Pamela Espeland.
        p. cm.
    Includes bibliographical references.
    ISBN 0-915793-44-X
    1. Sexual harassment of women—Study and teaching (Secondary)—United States.
2. Sexual harassment of women—United States—Prevention. I. Espeland, Pamela.
II. Title.
HQ1237.5.U6G66 1992
305.3—dc20   92-18013
                                                                                        CIP

Cover and book design by MacLean and Tuminelly

10 9 8 7 6 5 4 3 2 1

Printed in the United States of America

FREE SPIRIT PUBLISHING INC.
400 First Avenue North, Suite 616
Minneapolis, MN 55401
(612) 338-2068

Many of the examples in "Developing and Implementing Sexual Harassment Policy and Procedure" were developed with information from the Minnesota Department of Education, Sex Equity Division, and the Minnesota State School Boards Association.

Dear Reader:

Sexual Harassment and Teens is not about pointing fingers, instilling guilt, labeling people, or assigning liability. It is about addressing and solving any sexual harassment problems that may exist in your school or organization, putting an end to recurring problems, and creating a climate in which sexual harassment is unacceptable because it hurts people and because it is illegal.

This is first and foremost a proactive, preventive, *positive* program— a partnership between adults and teens working for change that will benefit everyone. While it contains information about relevant laws, it does not give legal advice. While it describes legal action as a recourse for sexual harassment, it is not intended as a how-to hand-book for instigating lawsuits against harassers. Rather, it is our sincere hope that this program will obviate many potential sexual harassment lawsuits by bringing people together in a cooperative, non-threatening way to address, explore, and understand the causes and consequences of this pervasive social problem.

We applaud your willingness to confront the issues presented in *Sexual Harassment and Teens*. Please let us know how this program works for you.

Judy Galbraith, President
Free Spirit Publishing
August 1992

DEDICATION

This book is dedicated to my daughters,
Amy and Jill
—S.S.

To John
—P.L.E.

ACKNOWLEDGMENTS

Some of the material in this work was originally produced and funded under a grant from Federal Title IV, provided by the U.S. Department of Education.

Portions of this work were originally developed under the auspices of and distributed by the Minnesota Department of Education, Equal Educational Opportunities Section, for whose support I am grateful.

Special thanks go to:

- Marcie Combs, a delightful colleague who shared in the development of the study and first drafts of the curriculum;

- Carver Scott Educational Cooperative, for providing the opportunity to examine this issue and conduct the study;

- My parents, Dr. Ken and Jean Strauss, for their love, encouragement, and teachings;

- My sister, Julie, for her telephone support;

- Tricia, Annie, Lois, and Penny for their friendship, support, and ability to challenge the status quo;

- Judy Galbraith, for her support and belief in the issue and the manuscript;

- Pamela Espeland, for her phenomenal writing expertise, support, and perseverance;

- The staff at Free Spirit; and

- My husband, Ed Hjermstad, for being there.

—Susan Strauss

CONTENTS

LIST OF REPRODUCIBLE PAGES

INTRODUCTION

ABOUT THE PROGRAM

Sexual Harassment and Teens is designed for use in junior high/middle schools and senior high schools—grades 7 through 12. It is an appropriate part of a course in social science, sociology, cultural awareness, vocational education, work study, human sexuality, and current events, among others. It is also recommended for use in churches, community groups, youth groups, workplaces, and anywhere sexual harassment of teens is a concern or a reality.

The program was developed as a result of studies conducted in Minnesota schools. When the curriculum was classroom tested, 61 percent of the males and 68 percent of the females felt that their assumptions about men and women had changed as a result of the course. The evaluation results were very positive, with student comments ranging from "interesting" to "educational" and "necessary."

One boy wrote, "I am guilty so I have stopped." Other boys said that they had learned to respect the opposite sex. Many girls reported, "I learned that I don't have to take it, and there is something I can do about it." One girl observed, "Yesterday I saw a guy corner a girl, and it made me see the situation differently than I normally would."

Without intervention, unhealthy sexual attitudes and behaviors formed before and during adolescence may go unchallenged and unchanged throughout life. Providing information about sexual harassment is a positive and effective form of intervention. *Sexual Harassment and Teens* gives young people a safe, supervised opportunity to examine their own attitudes and behaviors regarding gender roles and sexual harassment. For many teens, all it takes is a little education to bring about awareness, reflection, empathy, and changes in negative behaviors.

PROGRAM COMPONENTS

The *Sexual Harassment and Teens* curriculum consists of three units. Each unit includes the following components:

- descriptions of the unit objectives
- an approximate time requirement
- a list of resources and equipment needed
- suggested scripts
- student activities and discussions
- supplemental activities and materials, including discussion questions, and
- reproducible pages for making transparencies and handouts.

The units may be presented in three class periods of approximately 45–60 minutes each. Supplemental activities and materials are provided so you can expand the course beyond that time frame, if you choose. This allows you the flexibility to teach in the style you prefer, and to give more emphasis to a particular idea or concept presented in the curriculum.

If you do decide to present the program in three hours over just three days, the rate of delivery will be rapid, since there is a great deal of information to cover. For more about the time requirements, see page 35.

In addition to the units that comprise the curriculum, *Sexual Harassment and Teens* includes the following sections:

- "Perspectives on Sexual Harassment" (pages 3–22), designed as a "short course" on sexual harassment, considers its causes and effects, reviews relevant laws, gives examples, explores related issues, and more. Be sure to read this section before starting to teach the program. The information it contains will help you to present the units with greater confidence and authority.

- "Developing and Implementing Sexual Harassment Policy and Procedure" (pages 23–30) offers reasons and guidelines that will help you to create a policy for your school or district, and/or evaluate an existing policy for comprehensiveness and effectiveness.

- "25 Ways to Prevent Sexual Harassment" (pages 31–32) contains specific suggestions for supporting and enhancing the curriculum, making sexual harassment awareness and prevention part of everyday life in your school and community.

- "Getting Ready to Teach the Program" (pages 33–37) is self-explanatory; pay special attention to the "Ten Tips" on pages 35–36.

- The "Sexual Harassment Survey" (pages 134–138), the concluding activity in Unit Three, can also be used at other times to gather valuable information about sexual harassment in your school and community.

- The "Course Evaluation" (pages 139–140) helps you to collect and assess student responses to the *Sexual Harassment and Teens* curriculum. Use it to learn how your students' attitudes and perceptions have changed, and to identify any areas that may require further attention, discussion, and teaching.

This program includes a great deal of information about sexual harassment. If you wish to explore the topic in more detail, "Additional Readings and Resources" (pages 141–142) will point you toward books and articles, films and videos.

A NOTE ON THE LANGUAGE

Women and girls are the primary targets of sexual harassment, and *Sexual Harassment and Teens* reflects that fact. While nonsexist language is imperative in any educational program, this curriculum most often presents "she" as the victim and "he" as the harasser.

This isn't meant to imply that men and boys don't experience sexual harassment. Sometimes they do, and when they do it is just as dehumanizing and discriminatory as when it happens to women and girls.

YOUR FEEDBACK IS REQUESTED

Please let me know how *Sexual Harassment and Teens* works for you. Tell me your experiences in teaching the program, and your ideas for modifying and/or improving it. Share your stories and describe how your district deals with the problem of sexual harassment. You may write to me c/o Free Spirit Publishing Inc., 400 First Avenue North, Suite 616, Minneapolis, MN 55401. I look forward to hearing from you.

Susan Strauss
Fall 1992

PERSPECTIVES ON SEXUAL HARASSMENT

SEXUAL HARASSMENT AND TEENS

"I think high school is something that most kids look forward to—you see movies, read books about high school being the best time—and I'll always remember dark days, coming home, sitting on my bedroom floor sobbing."
—Katy [1]

Katy was a 15-year-old in a Minnesota high school when she learned that sexually explicit and degrading graffiti about her was appearing in a stall of one of the boys' bathrooms. The school dismissed her repeated complaints; the graffiti remained and proliferated.

Sexual harassment is a pervasive social problem among teenagers today, and it escalates when ignored. These are the two main conclusions we can draw from interviews with teenagers, and from existing studies that focus on sexual harassment and teens.

In response to a sexual harassment questionnaire distributed to student leaders from 13 school districts at a Minnesota State Sex Equity Student Leadership conference:

- 80 percent of the students said they were aware of sexual harassment in their schools

- 75 percent said they were aware of sexual harassment between students

- 50 percent said they were aware of sexual harassment between students and staff

- 26 percent said sexual harassment "goes on all the time"

- 50 percent said "it happens to a fair number of people"

- 6 percent said "it doesn't happen." [2]

Another study conducted at a Minnesota secondary vocational school surveyed 250 students from four school districts. Approximately 50 percent of the teenage girls reported having been verbally and physically harassed at school; another 30 percent stated that they had been harassed at work.

Although I found no statistical data specifically regarding the harassment of teenage boys in schools, stories are prevalent. They tell of boys harassing other boys as a "joke," of girls grabbing boys' genitals, and of both genders making comments about boys' sexuality and sexual prowess.

Whether male or female, teenagers tend to ignore sexual harassment when it happens to them. They feel pressured to put up with it and not cause trouble. They are afraid of being ridiculed and of losing popularity. They worry that people will think they are making a big deal out of nothing, or that others will blame them for provoking the harassment. If the harasser is a teacher, they fear that their grades will suffer if they don't go along.

Girls report feeling angry, confused, and ashamed immediately following sexual harassment incidents, and for a long time afterwards; sexual harassment is an experience with lasting harmful effects. They find their harassers disgusting—not, as some harassers mistakenly believe, sexually attractive. Many regret that they didn't do more to bring justice to the incident when it happened. Boys are often amazed to learn that their behavior is seen as a turn-off by girls.

Most sexual harassment of teenagers at school occurs among peers, student to student, in the classroom during class time, and in the hallways between classes. Harassers tend to have a reputation for harassing, which occurs on a continuum from sometimes to daily.

Anecdotal evidence points to many harassers being athletes—perhaps because of sexual stereotyping, and perhaps because athletes are more visible in the community. Athletes may or may not be more guilty of sexual harassment than non-athletes, but they are often the leaders in their schools, and they do serve as role models.

Of the students surveyed, many felt that sexual harassment problems in the school should be handled by the district, using legal means. They thought that teachers who harassed students should be fired. They believed that educational and support groups on the topic of sexual harassment should be offered to the schools and to the community as a whole. Most were unaware that the school was legally liable for sexual harassment occurring between students.

SEXUAL HARASSMENT AND THE LAW

"I couldn't handle it anymore. I came home and said, 'Mom, I'm sick of this. I'm sick of going to school every day and hearing this. I'm sick of getting no support from the school system. I'm going to do something about this because it's bothering me.'"
　　　　—Jill [3]

Jill was a senior at a Minnesota high school when she learned that her name appeared on a sexually explicit list being circulated through her school. She had endured different forms of sexual harassment since the eighth grade. When her complaints were ignored yet again, she charged her school district with sexual harassment through

the Minnesota Department of Human Rights. The Department found that the district had "created an environment that promoted sexual harassment." As of this writing, Jill and her school district are still negotiating a settlement.

Katy, whose complaints about the graffiti in the boys' bathroom went unheard by her school, was awarded $15,000 in the fall of 1991. The Minnesota Department of Human Rights found that her school's failure to take action had violated state sexual harassment laws, and they ordered the school to pay.

Minnesota schools are now required by law to have written sexual harassment policies. All schools must post their rules and consequences and include them in the student handbook. Since 1991, the Minnesota State High School League, which governs athletic and fine arts activities statewide, has been required by law to have a sexual harassment/violence policy and consequences for all students who participate in these activities. In April, 1992, the Minnesota Legislature approved spending over $1.5 million to teach students in grades K through 12 about anti-violence, including sexual harassment and sexual assault.

Minnesota is one of the few states that is aggressively implementing and enforcing sexual harassment laws within the schools. Other states will need to follow its example, because sexual harassment is illegal nationwide, not only in Minnesota.

• Sexual harassment is illegal according to Civil Rights Act Title IX of the Federal Education Amendments, which prohibits sexual harassment in education. Title IX may be enforced through private litigation, the Civil Rights federal office, or state departments of human rights. Under Title IX, educational institutions are required to maintain a grievance procedure which allows for prompt and equitable resolution of sex discrimination.

• Sexual harassment is also illegal according to Civil Rights Act Title VII, which prohibits sexual harassment in the workplace.

- In 1980, the EEOC issued its "Final Amendment to Guidelines on Discrimination Because of Sex." These guidelines defined sexual harassment as a form of sex discrimination and went on to say:

  "Unwelcome sexual advances, requests for sexual favors, and other verbal or physical conduct of a sexual nature constitutes sexual harassment when:

  1. submission to such conduct is made either explicitly or implicitly a term or condition of an individual's employment;

  2. submission to or rejection of such conduct by an individual is used as the basis for employment decisions affecting such individual; or

  3. such conduct has the purpose or effect of unreasonably interfering with an individual's work performance or creating an intimidating, hostile, or offensive working environment."

- In 1986, the United States Supreme Court identified two forms of sexual harassment: "quid pro quo" and "hostile environment."

  - "Quid pro quo" applies when a person in a power position—a boss or supervisor—makes decisions that affect an employee's job based on whether the employee complies with his or her sexual demands.

  - "Hostile environment" applies when the harassing behavior of anyone in the workplace—not only a boss or supervisor—causes the workplace to become hostile, intimidating, or offensive and unreasonably interferes with an employee's work.

- The National Advisory Council on Women's Educational Programs has defined sexual harassment as "the use of authority to emphasize the sexuality or sexual identity of a student in a manner which prevents or impairs that student's full enjoyment of educational benefits, climate or opportunities."

- The Office for Civil Rights, United States Department of Education, has stated that "sexual harassment consists of verbal or physical conduct of a sexual nature, imposed on the basis of sex, by an employee or agent of a recipient that denies, limits, provides differently, or conditions the provision of aid, benefits, services or treatment protected under Title IX."

- Within the last few years, our understanding of what constitutes sexually harassing behaviors has been expanded by the Minnesota Department of Human Rights (and perhaps others) to include the following, when based on gender considerations:

  - sabotaging a person's work/school efforts, assignments, or reputation

  - assigning a person less challenging or responsible duties

  - unequal application of discipline, work/school rules, and performance standards, and

  - repeatedly belittling, demeaning, or insulting a person.

- Today it is generally accepted that any type of unwelcome conduct directed toward an employee or student because of his or her gender may constitute sexual harassment.

LEGAL DECISIONS AFFECTING SEXUAL HARASSMENT

1964

Civil Rights Act Title VII prohibits sexual/racial discrimination at work.

1972

Civil Rights Act Title IX, Federal Education Amendments, prohibits sexual/racial discrimination against students and staff in education.

1980

The EEOC defines sexual harassment.

1980

Continental Can v. Minnesota court case determines that an employer and/or organization is liable for sexual harassment and must take prompt action to correct the problem.

1982

Huebschen v. Wisconsin Department of Health & Social Services court case determines that submission to sexual advances cannot be made a term of employment, and that an organization is liable for the actions of its supervisors.

1986

Meritor State Bank v. Vinson court case determines that sexual harassment is a form of sex discrimination under Title VII, and that allowing an environment of sexual harassment is unlawful.

1991

Ellison v. Brady court case rules that a "reasonable woman" (rather than the traditional "reasonable person") standard should be applied by juries and judges in considering sexual harassment cases.

1991

Robinson v. Jacksonville Shipyard Inc. court case determines that posting pornographic material at work is a type of sexual harassment and creates a hostile environment.

1991

The Civil Rights Act of 1991 states that a victim of sexual harassment can attempt to recover compensatory and punitive damages from his or her employer.

1991

In an out-of-court settlement, a high school in Duluth, Minnesota is ordered to pay $15,000 in damages to a student who was sexually harassed by her male peers.

1992

Franklin v. Gwinnett County Public Schools makes clear that students who suffer sexual harassment and other forms of sex discrimination can seek monetary damages from their schools and school officials for violating their civil rights.

1992

The Minnesota Court of Appeals decides that an employee need not complain at the time about sexual harassment on the job in order to sue later and collect damages from the employer. Their decision strengthens the position that employers are liable if they knew or should have known about harassment. It supports the growing sense of awareness of which behaviors are appropriate, and which are clearly inappropriate.

The statute of limitations for filing a sexual harassment claim may differ from state to state. Some states have their own antidiscrimination laws allowing for a longer statute of limitations—up to a year in Minnesota, for example. Federal employees must file a claim with the Equal Employment Opportunity Commission (EEOC) within 30 days from the date of the last sexual harassment incident; private sector employees have 180 days to bring a charge to the EEOC. Many people believe that the statute of limitations unfairly restricts victims who want to file charges, since it limits the time they have to weigh their options and make informed decisions.

The passage of the Civil Rights Act of 1991 meant that a victim of sexual harassment could attempt to recover compensatory and punitive damages from his or her employer. Prior to the passage of this act, victims were not able to collect damages under Title VII. It is expected that this will be applied and interpreted in different ways from case to case, and from company to company, with the number of employees being a determining factor.

The law indicates that isolated trivial incidents will not be cause for sexual harassment liability. The behavior must be severe or pervasive enough to create a hostile environment in the workplace or school.

In February, 1992, the United States Supreme Court unanimously ruled that students who suffer sexual harassment and other forms of sex discrimination can seek monetary damages from their schools and school officials for violating their civil rights.

Sexual harassment may also be a criminal offense under child abuse laws.

SEXUAL HARASSMENT IN THE SCHOOLS

"Personally, I don't really hear it in the halls at all."
"I don't see a lot of it."
　　　　—Male students at a Minnesota high school [4]

"What they yelled at me was, I have nice, firm breasts."
"It just boils down to basic disrespect."
　　　　—Female students at the same Minnesota high school [5]

Over the past several years, sexual harassment has been the focus of increasing attention on college campuses and in the workplace. Until recently, however, almost no attention has been paid to the sexual harassment that occurs in our junior high/middle and secondary schools.

As a result, most schools have done little or nothing about it. Harassing behaviors go unnoticed in the classroom. Students are not informed about ways to avoid harassment and defend their rights. Schools have become environments that support sexual harassment—in spite of the 1986 court ruling (*Meritor State Bank v. Vinson*) which clearly states that allowing such an environment is unlawful.

Many students say that sexual harassment is the norm in their schools.* There have been numerous reports of sexual assaults and rapes on school grounds and in school buildings. In an environment that condones sexual harassment, everyone is a victim, not just those who are direct targets of the harassment. All students come to see school as an unsafe place, hostile and intimidating. They may alter their own behaviors in an attempt to decrease their sense of vulnerability.

Often, administrators fail to take effective action, even when informed of specific occurrences of sexual harassment in their schools. Inappropriate behaviors are excused with such phrases as "That's just emerging adolescent sexuality," "Let them have their fun," or "Boys will be boys." This attitude only perpetuates the cycle of sexual harassment.

- A principal and a group of 25 parents were informed of a sexual assault that had occurred in their school. No one offered any comment about it; no one wanted to explore the option of investigating the complaint.

---

*Increasingly, it is not only students who are being harassed. Teachers and staff are being harassed, too—by students.

- A school board member refused to allow a sexual harassment curriculum to be implemented in his district because he didn't want "enlightened" students to know their rights. His reason: "They might sue us."

Studies have shown that sexual harassment is most likely to occur in organizations where management fails to implement a strong philosophy and policy indicating that such behaviors won't be tolerated. In other words, it's not only students who need to learn about sexual harassment. Administrators, teachers, support staff, janitors, bus drivers—all adults who have anything to do with school—should receive training in sexual harassment awareness and prevention.

If we teach students without teaching the adults, we cannot hope to effect the far-reaching systemic changes that are required to confront and solve the pervasive problem of sexual harassment.

THE SPECIAL NEEDS STUDENT

Special needs students offer additional challenges in dealing with sexual harassment in school. Mentally challenged students may be at greater risk of being sexually harassed by other students due to their increased vulnerability. Teens identified as EBD (Emotionally and Behaviorally Disturbed) may be more likely to become either victims or harassers.

EXAMPLES OF SEXUALLY HARASSING BEHAVIORS REPORTED IN U.S. HIGH SCHOOLS

- touching (arm, breast, buttock, etc.)
- verbal comments (about parts of the body, what type of sex the victim would be "good at," clothing, looks, etc.)
- name-calling (from "honey" to "bitch" and worse)
- spreading sexual rumors
- leers and stares
- sexual or "dirty" jokes
- cartoons, pictures, and pornography
- using the computer to leave sexual messages or graffiti or to play sexually offensive computer games
- gestures with the hands and body
- pressure for sexual activity
- cornering, blocking, standing too close, following
- conversations that are too personal
- "rating" an individual—for example, on a scale from 1 to 10
- obscene T-shirts, hats, pins
- showing R-rated movies during class
- "snuggies" (pulling underwear up at the waist so it goes in between the buttocks)
- sexual assault and attempted sexual assault
- rape
- massaging the neck, massaging the shoulders
- touching oneself sexually in front of others
- graffiti
- making kissing sounds or smacking sounds; licking the lips suggestively
- howling, catcalls, whistles
- repeatedly asking someone out when he or she isn't interested
- "spiking" (pulling down someone's pants)
- facial expressions (winking, kissing, etc.)
- "slam books" (lists of students' names with derogatory sexual comments written about them by other students)
- "making out" in the hallway.

A 1991 Minnesota Department of Education survey of 3,500 Minnesota teens who were either enrolled in alternative high schools, in treatment centers, or in the justice system found that two-thirds came from homes with multiple problems including sexual abuse, family violence, and chemical dependency. The males of this group were four times likelier to force sexual activity on their dates.[6]

The fact that these teens have been involved in abusive situations at home increases the likelihood that they will continue to be victims, and perhaps perpetrators, of verbal, physical, and sexual abuse in their relationships with friends and peers. Female sexual abuse victims often are more seductive in their dress and demeanor and more sexually active than their mainstream classmates. Male sexual abuse victims often act out sexually, becoming perpetrators themselves as a way of dealing with their own victimization. These young people feel a loss of power and self-esteem, and they are unclear about where their boundaries end and other people's begin.

While it is not appropriate to prejudge students because of their background and family origins, it is appropriate to set ground rules and consequences for specific

EXAMPLES OF SEXUAL HARASSMENT COMPLAINTS INVOLVING STUDENTS IN MINNESOTA SCHOOLS

Students, teachers, and parents have reported incidents and behaviors including:

- A group of male athletes dressed up as the girls from their school's dance line for a pep fest. Their costumes included signs worn in front of their genitals that read "suck me." Their actions were described as obscene and obnoxious as they "danced" in front of the students and faculty. This has been an annual event despite complaints from the faculty to the principal.

- The graphic, explicit R-rated movie "Angel Heart" was shown for two days in a high school classroom. A student complaint received no response.

- A boy's swim trunks were pulled down by two male "friends" at a coed swimming excursion sponsored by the school. No consequences were given to the two "friends."

- Eight high school boys gathered around a female classmate and pulled her skirt up over her head. The boys were told to write a letter of apology; none did, and no one from the administration or staff followed through.

- A girl was walking down the hallway when two boys, one on either side, grabbed her pants and pulled them down to her ankles.

- During a "powder puff" football game (at which the girls play football and the boys cheer), the male cheerleaders yelled cheers about the girls' "tits and ass" to the audience of students, staff, and parents.

- A boy was talking with a group of male and female friends when one of the girls grabbed his genitals and squeezed.

- A sophomore high school girl was raped by a classmate in the weight room of their high school.

- Female cheerleaders were lured into the back of a bus carrying their football team to an "away" game. The girls were urged to "show us what you girls are really for." They were told to sit on the floor of the bus so the players could have the seats to themselves.

- Three wrestlers sexually assaulted one of "their" cheerleaders during the state wrestling tournament.

behaviors, preferably at the beginning of the school year. If a special needs student appears to be prone to sexual harassment, it may be advisable to set up specific goals and objectives concerning such behavior in the student's IEP (Individual Education Plan).

While a student's EBD status may play a role in explaining harassing behavior, it is not an excuse for the behavior. These students should experience the same consequences as mainstream students.

The Fair Pupil Dismissal Act requires due process when a student is suspended, and a periodic review of the IEP to determine if the behavior that led to the suspension is related to the student's handicapping condition.

SEXUAL HARASSMENT IN THE WORKPLACE

When the *Harvard Business Review* surveyed its readers about sexual harassment in the workplace, one male respondent answered that "the [EEOC Sexual Harassment] guidelines will be hard to implement because of 41,000 years of habit."[7] This statement reflects one of the attitudes that keep sexual harassment alive in America's workplaces.

The Anita Hill-Clarence Thomas hearings of 1991 served as a national in-service on the subject of sexual harassment. For many people, the hearings illuminated the connection between sexual harassment and power.

Clarence Thomas wasn't only Anita Hill's boss; he was also the chief federal officer of the EEOC, the federal organization responsible for establishing the sexual harassment guidelines that function as the legal definition.

If Anita Hill was telling the truth—and people will long be debating both sides of this issue—her situation must have seemed hopeless in 1981, when the incidents allegedly occurred. Back then, most people had never even heard the phrase "sexual harassment"; although the behavior was ages old, the concept was relatively new. Had Anita Hill spoken out at the time, nobody would have believed her.

Ten years later, the Senate Judiciary Committee initially dismissed her charges, agreeing to hear them only after intense pressure from the American public. The all-male committee challenged Anita Hill's motives, credibility, even her sanity.

In the aftermath of the Hill-Thomas hearings, women are saying that they are angry and tired of being the gatekeepers of men's sexual behavior. They don't understand why men "just don't get it." Meanwhile, men are saying that they are concerned about being lumped together and unfairly accused. They don't enjoy being labeled "male animals" who can't control their sexual behavior.

Numerous studies have been conducted of sexual harassment in the workplace, and they have yielded similar results. Among the most widely publicized are the U.S. Merit Systems

---

CHARACTERISTICS OF ORGANIZATIONS AT RISK FOR SEXUAL HARASSMENT

Organizations where sexual harassment is most likely to occur are those in which:

- there is no sexual harassment policy and procedure
- sexual harassment policy and procedure exist but are not visibly supported or disseminated

- jobs are traditionally all-male or all-female
- there is limited information from the bottom up
- there are no consequences for harassers
- there is no formal training in sexual harassment.

HOW SEXUAL HARASSMENT AFFECTS THE ORGANIZATIONAL ENVIRONMENT

Sexual harassment creates an intimidating, hostile, or offensive environment in which:

- people develop morale problems
- they are less trusting
- they are less productive

- they are confused and bewildered
- they do not feel safe
- they feel angry toward the organization
- relations between people are hostile
- women and men are polarized
- the organization feels like a dangerous place to be.

Protection Board surveys of 1980 and 1988, which focused on sexual harassment among federal government employees nationwide.

The 1980 survey found that:

- 42 percent of women experienced sexual harassment
- 15 percent of men experienced sexual harassment
- 52 percent of those who experienced sexual harassment quit or were fired because of the harassment.

The 1988 survey also found that 42 percent of women government employees were harassed. The most common harassing behaviors included sexual teasing, jokes, remarks, looks/leers, gestures, touching, leaning over/cornering, and pinching.

Other studies of sexual harassment in the workplace indicate that more than 42 percent of women are being sexually harassed. "Facts on Sexual Harassment," a publication of the NOW Legal Defense and Education Fund, maintains that 50–75 percent of working women experience sexual harassment. The U.S. Army reports that three out of four women in the army are sexually harassed. Women and men in nontraditional jobs are victimized more often, especially women in construction, investment banking, and medicine—specifically, women surgeons.

Two new and unprecedented sexual harassment cases have been made public during this writing. In Minnesota, five women have

filed sexual harassment suits against Stroh's Brewery, alleging that they were subjected to verbal and physical harassment by their male colleagues and supervisors.

What makes this case remarkable is that the women are charging that Stroh's advertising —which featured the Swedish Bikini Team— helped to create the hostile, intimidating, and offensive work environment at the company. The women allege that they were subjected to lewd comments, unwanted touches, and degrading posters at work, and that they were harassed outside of work as well: their tires were slashed and damaged, and they were followed and harassed while driving down the highway.

The second unprecedented case involves female miners in Minnesota who are bringing a class-action suit alleging sexual harassment by the male miners they work with. A class-action suit requires that all people in the "class"—in this instance, women—claim to have experienced the same treatment. Previous sexual harassment cases have involved individuals or small groups; obviously this case is much broader.

The women miners claim that they were touched, pinched, grabbed, and kissed against their will, and that posters, drawings, and photos degrading to women were posted around their workplace, including the lunchroom, tool room, lockers, desks, offices, the women's vehicles, elevators, women's restrooms, in interoffice mail, and on the company bulletin boards.

The financial costs of sexual harassment are significant. In 1987, the federal government estimated the indirect costs of sexual harassment at $267 million over a two-year period in lost productivity, turnover, and absenteeism. According to a 1988 survey of Fortune 500 companies by *Working Woman* magazine, sexual harassment costs the typical company $6.7 million a year in those same indirect costs.[8]

For many women, the decision to lodge a formal complaint may be an economic one. Loss of one's job and benefits, and/or the need to hire an attorney who demands high fees (because these cases are difficult to win), are but a few of the costs a woman must be willing to incur. The only time the EEOC provides free legal help is when the agency itself takes the case to court, which is unusual. In 1990, the EEOC received 5600 charges of sexual harassment and took only 50 of these cases to court.

The Civil Rights Act of 1964 states that a claimant who wins a case is entitled to reinstatement of his or her job with back pay. The new Civil Rights Act of 1991 allows the victim of sexual harassment to claim compensatory and punitive damages, up to a maximum amount that depends on the size of the company. For example, if the company has 16 to 100 employees, a victim may claim damages up to $50,000; if the company has over 500 employees, a victim may claim damages up to $300,000.

Such ceilings are imposed only for victims of sexual discrimination (which includes sexual harassment) and disabled persons; victims of other civil rights violations—race, color, or national origin—have no such ceiling for the amount of damages that may be awarded. Since the majority of sexual discrimination charges are brought by women, it can be argued that this in itself is a form of discrimination under the civil rights law.

Most victims of sexual harassment in the workplace never file complaints. Of the 57 percent of female and male federal government employees who experienced harassment, as reported in the Merit Systems Protection Board surveys, only five percent filed complaints. Those who did reported that the process was

slow and burdensome, and often the harasser was also the investigator.

The majority of women who have filed sexual harassment complaints at their workplace say that filing had serious negative ramifications. These included reprisal, alienation from their colleagues, and stress-related physical and emotional consequences.

Furthermore, interviewers may ask job applicants if they have ever filed a discrimination suit against a previous employer. If the answer is "yes," there is the risk of not getting hired.

UNDERSTANDING AND SUPPORTING THE VICTIM

"You may laugh or something because you're nervous and people are looking at you, but it does bother you—it affects your self-esteem."
　　　　—Female student [9]

"It makes you feel less than the person you are."
　　　　—Female student [10]

"No, I do not enjoy it. I mean, it's my body."
　　　　—Male student [11]

Most victims of sexual harassment—women and men, adults and teens—just try to ignore it, hoping it will stop. In fact, ignoring harassment usually exacerbates it.

Women sometimes appear to go along with their harassers, joking and giggling even when they are offended or afraid. If they get angry enough or frustrated enough, they may confront their harassers; some studies have indicated that women are more likely to do this than men.

Although an assertive response is almost always more effective than a passive response, a firm "NO" may not be enough, especially if power is the motive behind the harassment. As a next step, some victims take an informal resolution approach, writing a letter to the harasser or asking another person to speak to the harasser on the victim's behalf.[12] A formal complaint is usually a last resort, made only when the harassment has become intolerable. Most teenagers never complain at all.

Many victims never report incidents of sexual harassment because they fear reprisal or retaliation, or they assume that reporting won't do any good. One study showed that 41 percent of victims felt that reporting made the harassment worse, and nothing happened to the harasser.

Victims undergo various stages of grieving in response to their experience, much like the stages an individual passes through following the death of a loved one. The intensity of each stage may vary, depending on the severity of the harassment.

- The first stage—a combination of shock, denial, and fear that may last anywhere from weeks to months—is characterized by refusal to acknowledge that the harassment occurred; inability or unwillingness to show emotions about the harassment; feelings of insecurity; and the fear of being alone.

- The second stage—anger—is characterized by intense feelings of anger and rage; the desire to get even; reliving the experience; mood swings; nightmares; psychosomatic complaints (65 percent have headaches, ulcers, backaches, etc.); irritability; withdrawal (a symptom of anger turned inward); self-blame; shame; feelings of powerlessness; increased absenteeism from school or work; decreased productivity; and loss of self-esteem.

- During the third stage—resolution—the victim begins to integrate the experience into her life. Although it is not forgotten, it becomes less predominant.

Much of how a victim feels about herself may depend on how others treat her—whether they believe her or dismiss her, support her or discredit her. Our society tends to blame the victim for everything from theft to rape. If somebody's car is burglarized, we ask, "Was it locked?" If a person is injured in an automobile collision with a drunk driver, we want to know, "Were you wearing your seat belt?"

If a woman is sexually harassed or assaulted, we wonder where she was, what she was wearing, what she was doing, and what she said to provoke her attacker. A 1991 poll by the Minneapolis *Star Tribune* showed that, nationally, 57 percent of men and 48 percent of women believe that rape victims share some of the blame.[13]

Blaming the victim removes all responsibility from the harasser. It also decreases our own sense of vulnerability. As University of Minnesota sociologist Candace Kruttschnidt observes, "If you can't ascribe blame to the victim, then it can happen to anybody and that's frightening. Being able to distance yourself from the event [by attributing it to the way the victim acted or dressed] gives you a lot of relief. If there is nothing she could have done [to prevent the rape], it is much more frightening."[14] In essence, we say to ourselves, "I don't (dress like that, wear that makeup, walk down that street, stay out late at night, etc.), therefore *it can't happen to me.*"

Victims may even blame themselves—partly due to social conditioning, and partly because this allows them to take back some control over the event. If they don't repeat the behavior that "got them in trouble," they can avoid getting in trouble again. According to author Robin Warshaw in her book, *I Never Called It Rape*, only 27 percent of women who have been raped think of themselves as rape victims. Acknowledging their experience would require them to confront their own vulnerability.

Blaming the victim perpetuates the cycle of sexual violence. It prevents the victim from reporting the incident, and it permits society to keep the issue at bay by labeling it the victim's problem rather than society's problem.

If society won't support the victim, we as individuals can. Barbara Chester, a specialist on the subject of victimization, offers the following recommendations:

- Define the victim's experience as sexual harassment.

- Assure confidentiality.

- Recognize the victim's sense of grief and loss.

- Provide a safe environment for the victim.

- Affirm the victim.

HOW SEXUAL HARASSMENT AFFECTS THE VICTIM

Physical Effects

Stress-related physical symptoms and problems including:

- acne
- changes in body weight
- colds
- dependence on alcohol or other drugs
- headaches/stomach aches/backaches/other physical aches and pains
- illness
- loss of appetite/eating disorders
- nausea
- sleeplessness/sleep disturbances
- sore throats
- ulcers

Emotional Effects

- anger
- anxiety
- confusion
- depression
- detachment
- embarrassment
- fear
- feeling degraded
- feeling intimidated
- feeling powerless
- feelings of dread
- guilt
- hopelessness
- humiliation
- irritability
- isolation/withdrawal
- loss of trust in others
- low self-esteem
- mood swings
- self-blaming
- self-doubt
- shame
- stress

School Performance/Experience Effects

- absenteeism
- "acting out" (behaving inappropriately to get attention)
- damaged reputation
- delayed graduation
- drop in quality of school work
- dropping a class
- dropping out of school
- inability to concentrate/feeling distracted
- loss of friends
- loss of trust in the educational system
- lower grades
- switching classes
- switching schools
- tardiness
- truancy

Future Effects

- continued inability to trust others
- continued stress-related physical problems and symptoms
- loss of job recommendations
- loss of recommendations for college admission or other post-secondary education
- loss of career and job opportunities
- loss of economic opportunities

Job-Related Effects

- loss of income
- loss of one's job and employee benefits including unemployment insurance
- loss of promotional opportunities and job-related educational opportunities
- loss of job skills
- reassignment
- dread of work
- distraction from tasks
- inability to work
- drop in work quality
- loss of job recommendations
- absenteeism
- tardiness

- Provide choices so the victim regains some sense of empowerment. (Examples: "Which hospital would you like to go to?" "Are you ready to call the police?")

- Don't force the victim to make decisions.

- Listen respectfully.

- Be nonjudgmental.

- Validate the victim's feelings and worth.

- Reinforce that it is not the victim's fault.

- Respect the victim's personal timing regarding her/his ability to cope.

- Familiarize yourself with outside agencies so you can refer the victim for counseling.[15]

SEXUAL HARASSMENT VS. FLIRTING

"I talk to young men and say, 'Listen, would you want this happening to your younger sister? Would you want this happening to your mother when she was a young lady in high school?'"
  —Minnesota Attorney General "Skip" Humphrey [16]

Sexual harassment is an ambiguous group of behaviors, which accounts for a large part of the problem. Whether harassment has occurred is truly in the "eye of the beholder"—or the ear. Some people may consider "Hey, babe," as a harmless, flirtatious comment, while others may see it as sexual harassment. The deciding factor is the feelings a particular phrase, gesture, or behavior evokes in the individual on the receiving end.

Students surveyed over a period of years have shared their own ideas about feelings and perceptions created by sexual harassment and flirting; their contributions are summarized in the lists on page 16. It's important to recognize that the same words and actions may evoke opposite feelings in different people.

Because sexual harassment can have severe legal consequences, there is a genuine fear of giving a compliment and having it misinterpreted as sexual harassment. How can we

tell the right from the wrong thing to say or do? How can we determine if our comments and behaviors are wanted or unwanted?

Actually, there is a fairly easy way to do this. We can ask ourselves a few simple questions:

1. Would I want my comments and/or behaviors to appear in the newspaper or on TV so my family and friends would know about them?

2. Is this something I would say or do if my mother or father, girlfriend or boyfriend, sister or brother, wife or husband were present?

3. Is this something I would want someone else to say or do to my mother or father, girlfriend or boyfriend, sister or brother, wife or husband?

4. Is this something I would say or do if the other person's significant other (wife, husband, boyfriend, girlfriend) were present?

5. Is there a difference in power between me and the other person? (Am I that person's teacher, supervisor, or employer, or do I have power over that person for some other reason? Examples: size, social status, etc.)

DIFFERENT GENDERS, DIFFERENT PERCEPTIONS

"I think some people are taking this issue real sensitive....They're making it out to be bigger than it really is."
  —Male student [17]

"Most men...have not been on the receiving end of sexual harassment....Because the problem is not theirs, many claim there is no problem."
  —Female student [18]

Men and women perceive sexual attention differently. In a survey of 1,000 men and women in Los Angeles, 67 percent of the men said that they would be "complimented" if they were propositioned, as compared to 17 percent of the women.[19]

SEXUAL HARASSMENT VS. FLIRTING

SEXUAL HARASSMENT
makes the receiver feel:

bad

angry/sad

demeaned

ugly

powerless

SEXUAL HARASSMENT
results in:

negative self-esteem

SEXUAL HARASSMENT
is perceived as:

one-sided

demeaning

invading

degrading

SEXUAL HARASSMENT is:

unwanted

power-motivated

illegal

FLIRTING
makes the receiver feel:

good

happy

flattered

pretty/attractive

in control

FLIRTING
results in:

positive self-esteem

FLIRTING
is perceived as:

reciprocal

flattering

open

a compliment

FLIRTING is:

wanted

equality-motivated

legal

This difference in perception is reflected in the "reasonable woman" standard determined in January 1991 by U.S. Ninth Circuit Court of Appeals Judge Robert Beezer. Historically, the courts had applied the "reasonable person" standard to cases of sexual harassment. Judge Beezer ruled that "a sex-blind reasonable person standard tends to be male-biased and tends to systematically ignore the experiences of women. What might appear trivial behavior to a man could be frightening or upsetting to a woman."[20]

Michelle Paludi, a psychologist at Hunter College, surveyed men and women to find out their perceptions of when sexual harassment occurred in the following scenario: [21]

A woman professor at a university was invited to lunch by her department chair to discuss research. Research was not the topic during lunch; rather, the professor was questioned about her personal life. After a few lunches, he asked her to dinner and drinks and then tried to fondle her.

Most of the women Paludi surveyed said that the sexual harassment began at lunch, when the department chair started asking the professor personal questions. But most of the men said that it began with the fondling.

Researchers who surveyed college students at Pennsylvania State University found that while dressing attractively, going to a party, sharing a drink, casual touching, and even telling a suggestive joke are perceived by women as friendly, fun behaviors, men are likely to interpret them as evidence of sexual interest.[22]

Misunderstandings like these can lead to inappropriate and even harassing behaviors. Both men and women would benefit from learning how to communicate clearly and how to question their own assumptions, especially when interpreting cues received from others.

POWER, STEREOTYPES, GENDER BIAS, AND VIOLENCE

"Guys grab themselves and say, 'Yo, baby, you know you want this.'"
"Society treats women as second class—that's why this happens. It's a symptom of a bigger problem."
"Although there are many young men who can see women as equals, there are those who regard females as hallway entertainment."
       —Female students [23]

"It's a man thing. When a girl has on something revealing, you have to say something about it....If the girl doesn't tell us we're sexually harassing her, we're going to continue to do it."
       —Male student [24]

Sexual harassment is not about sexual attraction. It is about power—more specifically, the misuse and abuse of power.

John Gottman, a psychologist at the University of Washington, observes that "sexual harassment is a subtle rape and rape is more about fear than sex...a way for a man to make a woman vulnerable."[25]

Louise Fitzgerald, a psychologist at the University of Illinois, states that about 25 percent of sexual harassment cases are actually botched seductions, less than 5 percent involve bribes or threats for sex, and the remaining 70 percent are assertions of power. This includes both *formal power*, which comes from being in a position of authority (employers, principals, and teachers have formal power), and *informal power*, which is given to males by our culture.[26]

From childhood on, many males in our culture are taught to be controlling, competitive, and aggressive—powerful when compared to females. In contrast, females are taught to be passive, nurturing, and supportive—powerless when compared to males.

The sex-role stereotyping of women as weak and men as sexual predators with out-of-control libidos supports and sustains sexual harassment, which may be a way for men to bond with other men. A man who refuses to go along with harassing behavior may find his sexuality called into question.

By adolescence, if not earlier, females in our culture have internalized sex-role stereotypes and started living by their rules. Consciously or not, they are aware that:

- females are valued less by our society
- males and male interests get more attention
- females are paid less, and their work is considered less important
- violence towards females is accepted and acceptable (as evident from television, video games, rock and rap music, music videos, pornography, advertising, and movies)
- females' contributions to science, art, and history are not recognized
- males are the TV heroes
- news stories center around men's experience of the world
- male sports merit TV coverage; female sports do not
- "he" can mean both "he and she," but "she" cannot
- and so on.

Studies show that female students face gender bias in the classroom starting as early as first grade. According to the American Association of University Women (AAUW), boys are:

- more likely to get attention from the teacher
- more likely to call out in class
- more likely to demand help, and
- more likely to be praised by the teacher.[27]

Boys out-talk girls in the classroom at a ratio of three to one. While boys are praised for the content and quality of their work, girls are praised for the neatness of theirs. When boys need help understanding an assignment or a problem, the teacher gives them more detailed directions; when girls need help, the teacher is more likely to do the work for them. Boys get more attention for being disruptive, and they are offered more school sports opportunities.

These subtle differences in how girls are treated add up to lower their self-esteem. The AAUW has found that girls' self-esteem continues to drop during their school years, resulting in lowered aspirations and expectations. A national study of 3,000 males and females showed that the self-esteem of both genders was about equal until puberty; by high school, the girls' self-esteem had dropped significantly more than the males.

Interestingly, the self-esteem of African-American girls dropped very little from junior high/middle school to high school as compared to that of Caucasian and Hispanic girls. The African-American girls apparently maintain their self-esteem by disassociating themselves from their schools—which, in turn, leads to poor academic performance.[28]

There also appears to be a correlation between self-esteem and how well girls do in math and science. The higher their self-esteem, the better they do in those traditionally "male" courses.

A study of 36,000 Minnesota seventh through twelfth graders by the Minnesota Department of Education and the Minnesota Department of Health found that females have a rougher time during adolescence than males. Because they are less disruptive than boys, they are easier to ignore. Because they feel they can't turn to adults for help, the adults remain unaware of their distress. Girls feel more alienated from their families than boys do. When faced with problems, they turn inward in self-destructive ways. According to the study:

- girls are nine times more likely than boys to have eating disorders

- their body image is three times lower than that of boys

- their stress level is one and one-half times higher

- their suicide risk is twice as high.[29]

In addition, girls are four times as likely as boys to have been physically and/or sexually abused.

Other studies indicate that one in three females, and one in seven males, will be victims of sexual abuse by age 18; that adult women have a one in four chance of being sexually assaulted during their lifetime; that every 15 seconds, a woman in the United States is beaten by her significant other; and that three to four million women are abused each year.

Rape in America: A Report to the Nation was released on April 21, 1992 by the National Victim Center, a crime victims rights group. According to that report, rape is five times more common than was previously thought. Other appalling findings reported in *Rape in America* include:

- Some 683,000 women are raped in the United States each year—one every 46 seconds. (The Justice Department reported 207,610 rapes in 1991.)

- One out of every eight American women has been raped at least once, bringing the number of current victims to over 12 million.

- 61 percent of victims are raped before age 18. Of these, 32 percent are raped between ages 11 and 17; 29 percent of the victims are under 11 years old.

- Half of rape victims are afraid of being killed or seriously injured during the rape.

- Three out of four rapists are friends or relatives of the victim; only 22 percent are strangers.

- Only 16 percent of rapes are ever reported.[30]

Rape is an act of violence; sexual harassment falls on the same continuum. Ours is a society that allows and even promotes violence. We have the highest homicide rate in the world. We lead the industrial world in death row executions. Six out of ten American couples are in violent relationships, resulting in 30,000 emergency room visits each year and 100,000 days of hospitalization; the leading cause of injury among women is being beaten by a man at home. Students bring approximately 95,000 weapons into our schools every day.[31]

The media have turned violence into entertainment, making real-life incidents seem ordinary and insignificant. Dr. Brandon Centerwall, a psychiatric researcher at the University of Washington, estimates that the influence of video violence may contribute to 10,000 murders and 70,000 rapes a year in the United States. Other studies are finding similar results in linking exposure to violent entertainment with aggressive and violent behavior.[32]

The American Psychological Association warns that "repeated exposure of scenes of violence against women in movies and TV creates a callousness toward women in both males and females." Dr. John Briere of the University of Southern California School of Medicine has found a relationship between aggression and the belief that violence is an acceptable way to dominate those with less power.[33]

In a cross-cultural study of rape, Peggy Reeves Sanday, a researcher at the University of Pennsylvania, found that violence-prone cultures are based on a dominance-submission system where sexual separation is the norm, with men having significantly more power than women.[34]

A study by Dr. Eva Feindler, Director of the Psychological Service Center at C.W. Post Long Island University in Brookville, New York, found that 30 to 40 percent of adolescent females are hit by their male dates. Even if these girls have a healthy relationship with their parents, they often do not tell them about these incidents. Rather, many of the girls claim that such violent behavior is "normal" and "a sign of love."[35] Other studies indicate that date violence is escalating.

In *I Never Called It Rape*, Robin Warshaw reports on a 1982 survey of college men. Sixty-one percent admitted to having forced a female into a type of sexual touching; one in twelve had committed acts that met the legal definition of rape or attempted rape. In other studies, 20 to 60 percent of high school and college males said that they would use force to get sex.

"We have created an epidemic of sexual disorders by having antisexual attitudes toward normal sexual development," says John Money, a sexologist at Johns Hopkins.[36] The onset for deviant sexual behavior is usually adolescence, often young adolescence or pre-teen. If a sex offender starts offending as a teen, he will have approximately 380 victims in his lifetime; if he starts after age 18, he will have approximately 20 victims. According to Michael O'Brien, a specialist working with adolescent sex offenders in Minnesota, rape is the most common violent crime committed by youths in the state.[37]

Facts like these clearly indicate the need for early intervention. We need to teach people how to protect themselves. Even more important, we need to teach potential perpetrators how to stop—or never start.

The roots of sexual violence may lie in what used to be called "typical adolescent behaviors" but are now recognized as sexual harassment. Or perhaps the rise in sexual harassment is a product of the violence in our society. Or maybe it's a vicious cycle, and if we eliminate one, we also eliminate the other.

THE PROMISE OF POSITIVE CHANGE

The sexual harassment of teens in our schools is dehumanizing and illegal. For the victim, its effects are far-reaching and debilitating.

As stated in *Who's Hurt and Who's Liable: Sexual Harassment in Massachusetts Schools*, "Sexual harassment in the educational setting is more than an uncomfortable situation resulting from the trials and tribulations of adolescent sexuality. Rather, it is an experience that interferes with a young woman's access to the education of her choice, and therefore seriously threatens her future occupation."

Change begins when even one individual—preferably a teacher, administrator, or staff person—becomes aware of the problem. That individual functions as a catalyst, heightening the awareness of his or her peers. From there, the domino effect takes over, and the entire school staff becomes informed. As the staff grows more knowledgeable and understanding, they begin to take a more proactive stance against sexual harassment, and the school climate grows progressively safer, healthier, and more open.

This process takes time and energy. Learning about sexual harassment is the easy part. Changing behaviors is more difficult, and changing attitudes is tougher still. Be patient and persistent. With individual change comes organizational change. It won't happen overnight—even in healthy organizations, organizational change can take from two to five years—but it will happen. The final step is a giant leap toward societal change. When that occurs, you can close this book, because you won't need it anymore.

NOTES

1. "Sexual Harassment 101."

2. Susan Strauss, "Sexual Harassment in the Schools."

3. "Sexual Harassment 101."

4. Ibid.

5. Ibid.

6. Jean Hopfensperger, "For Most Troubled Teens, Troubles Started at Home."

7. E.G. Collins and T.B. Bladgett, "Sexual Harassment...Some See It...Some Won't."

8. Ronni Sandroff, "Sexual Harassment in the Fortune 500."

9. "Insights in Ink."

10. Ibid.

11. Ibid.

12. An informal resolution approach that includes writing a letter to the harasser is described in Unit Three, pages 101–102. This technique was inspired by a section titled "Send a Letter to the Harasser" in *Who's Hurt and Who's Liable: Sexual Harassment in Massachusetts Schools*, which credits Mary P. Rowe, Ph.D., for developing it originally. See Mary P. Rowe, "Ideas for Action: Dealing with Sexual Harassment" in *Harvard Business Review* 59:3 (May–June 1991): 42–46.

13. Donna Halvorson, "Our Cultural Values Add to the Problem."

14. Ibid.

15. Barbara Chester, "Victimization."

16. "Sexual Harassment 101."

17. Ibid.

18. "Insights in Ink."

19. Barbara Gutek, *Sex and the Workplace.*

20. The Carter Institute, *The Ten Most Costly Mistakes Managers Make in Handling Sex Discrimination.*

21. Daniel Goleman, "Harassment: Not Sex but Power."

22. Antonia Abbey, "Misperceptions of Friendly Behavior as Sexual Interest."

23. "Insights in Ink."

24. Ibid.

25. Daniel Goleman, "Harassment: Not Sex but Power."

26. Ibid.

27. American Association of University Women, *How Schools Shortchange Girls.*

28. Ibid.

29. Minnesota Women's Fund, *Reflections of Risk.*

30. "Rape Study: Only 16% Are Reported."

31. Colman McCarthy, "Breaking the Cycle of Violence."

32. Noel Holston, "Police Officers Campaign to 'Turn Off the Violence.'"

33. League of Women Voters of Minneapolis, "Breaking the Cycle of Violence."

34. Peggy Reeves Sanday, "The Socio-Cultural Context of Rape: A Cross-Cultural Study."

35. Lawrence Kutner, "Teen Often Cannot End Abusive Relationship."

36. League of Women Voters of Minneapolis, "Breaking the Cycle of Violence."

37. Becky Montgomery, et al., *SHARP Curriculum.*

REFERENCES

"Definition of Harassment Expanded." *Training* (November 1991): 13, 50.

"42% of Women Working for U.S. Cite Harassment." *Washington Post*, as cited in Minneapolis *Star Tribune* (June 30, 1988).

"Insights in Ink." Minneapolis *Star Tribune* Newspaper and Education Department (March 27, 1992).

"Rape Study: Only 16% Are Reported." Minneapolis *Star Tribune* (April 24, 1992).

"School Administrators Can Be Sued for Overlooking Sexual Harassment by Staff." *School Law News* (September 28, 1989): 20.

Who's Hurt and Who's Liable: Sexual Harassment in Massachusetts Schools: A Curriculum and Guide for School Personnel. 4th Edition. Prepared for the Chapter 622 Team by Freada Klein, Consultant and Principal Co-Author; Nancy Wilber, Consultant and Principal Co-Author; Nan D. Stein, Ed.D., Product Developer/Editor; Sandra Moody, Esq., Legal Counsel; and Jana Kendall Harrison, Editor. Quincy: Massachusetts Department of Education, Division of Curriculum and Instruction, 1986.

"Why Women Don't Come Forward." *Feminist Majority Report* 3 (Fall/Winter 1991): 7.

Abbey, Antonia. "Misperceptions of Friendly Behavior as Sexual Interest: A Survey of Naturally Occurring Incidents." *Psychology of Women Quarterly* 1 (June 1987): 173–194.

Abel, Gene, Judy Becker, *et al. The Treatment of Child Molesters: A Manual.* New York: New York State Psychiatric Institute, Sexual Behavior Clinic, 1984.

Albee, George. *Promoting Sexual Responsibility and Preventing Sexual Problems.* Sol Gordon and Harold Leitenberg, eds. Hanover: University Press of New England, 1983.

American Association of University Women. *How Schools Shortchange Girls.* Washington, DC.: AAUW, 1992.

Carbonell, Joyce Lynn, *et al.* "Sexual Harassment of Women in the Workplace: Managerial Strategies for Understanding, Preventing and Limiting Liability." In *1990 Annual: Developing Human Resources,* 225–239. San Diego: University Associates, 1990.

The Carter Institute. *The Ten Most Costly Mistakes Managers Make in Handling Sex Discrimination.* Minneapolis: The Carter Institute, 1991.

Chester, Barbara. "Victimization," unpublished paper. Cited in Minnesota Curriculum Services Center, *Sexual Harassment: Facilitators Curriculum Manual,* below.

Chung, Jenny, and Nancy Turner. "Sexual Harassment Pervasive." *Feminist Majority Report* 3 (Fall/Winter 1991): 4.
— "Sexual Harassment: The Laws, History and Flaws." *Feminist Majority Report* 3 (Fall/Winter 1991): 5–6.

Collins, E. G., and T.B. Bladgett. "Sexual Harassment...Some See It...Some Won't." *Harvard Business Review* 59 (March–April 1981): 76–95.

Conroy, Mary. "Sexism in Our Schools: Training Girls for Failure." *Better Homes and Gardens* (February 1988): 44, 46, 48.

Diaz, Kevin. "Delinquent Girls: Lost Wards of State." Minneapolis *Star Tribune* (November 21, 1991).

Feshback, Seymour, and Neil Malamuth. "Sex and Aggression: Proving the Link." *Psychology Today* (November 1978): 110–112, 114, 116–117, 122.

Goleman, Daniel. "Harassment: Not Sex but Power." Minneapolis *Star Tribune* (October 26, 1991).

Gutek, Barbara. *Sex and the Workplace: The Impact of Sexual Behavior and Harassment on Women, Men, and Organizations.* New York: Jossey-Bass, 1985.

Halvorson, Donna. "Our Cultural Values Add to the Problem." Minneapolis *Star Tribune* (November 12, 1991).

Holston, Noel. "Police Officers Campaign to 'Turn Off the Violence.'" Minneapolis *Star Tribune* (September 29, 1991).

Hopfensperger, Jean. "For Most Troubled Teens, Troubles Started at Home." Minneapolis *Star Tribune* (September 21, 1991).
— and Paul McEnroe. "Confusion Exists on Issue of Harassing." Minneapolis *Star Tribune* (October 13, 1991).

Illinois Task Force on Sexual Harassment and Sangamon State University. *Task Force Survey Reported to Illinois House Judiciary Committee, March 4, 1980.* Springfield: Sangamon State University, 1980.

Kutner, Lawrence. "Teen Often Cannot End Abusive Relationship." Minneapolis *Star Tribune* (November 21, 1991).

League of Women Voters of Minneapolis. "Breaking the Cycle of Violence: A Focus on Primary Prevention Efforts." Minneapolis: League of Women Voters of Minneapolis, 1990.

Malamuth, Neil. "Rape Proclivity Among Men." *Journal of Social Issues* 4 (Fall 1981): 138–157.

McCarthy, Colman. "Breaking the Cycle of Violence." Minneapolis *Star Tribune* (October 31, 1991).

Minnesota Curriculum Services Center. *Sexual Harassment: Facilitators Curriculum Manual.* White Bear Lake: Minnesota Curriculum Services Center, 1987.

Minnesota Women's Fund. *Reflections of Risk: Growing Up Female in Minnesota: A Report on the Health and Well-being of Adolescent Girls in Minnesota.* Minneapolis: Minnesota Women's Fund, 1990.

Montgomery, Becky, *et al. SHARP (Sexual Health And Responsibility Program) Curriculum.* St. Paul: Minnesota Department of Human Services, 1986, 1988.

National Organization of Women Legal Defense and Education Fund. "Facts on Sexual Harassment." Washington, DC: NOW, 1985.

Pogrebin, Letty Cottin. "Boys Will Be Boys?" *MS.* (September 1989): 24.

Russell, Diana. *Sexual Exploitation.* Beverly Hills: Sage Publications Inc., 1984.

Sadker, Myra, and David Sadker. "Sexism in the Schoolroom of the 80's." *Psychology Today* (March 1985): 54, 56, 57.

Sanday, Peggy Reeves. "The Socio-Cultural Context of Rape: A Cross-Cultural Study." *Journal of Social Issues* 37 (Fall 1981): 5–27.

Sandroff, Ronni. "Sexual Harassment in the Fortune 500." *Working Woman* (December 1988): 69–73.

Schmidt, Laurie. *Effective Management Series: Preventing Sexual Harassment.* Minneapolis: Chrysalis: A Center for Women, 1982.

Soley, Ginney. "Our Lives at Stake: The Cultured Roots of Violence," unpublished report. Cited in League of Women Voters of Minneapolis, "Breaking the Cycle of Violence," above.

Strauss, Susan. "Sexual Harassment in the Schools: Legal Implications for Principals." *NASSP Bulletin* 72 (March 1988): 93–97.

Television news programs:

"ABC News with Peter Jennings," February 11, 1992.

"Sexual Harassment 101," special report, KARE-TV, Minneapolis-St. Paul, April 22, 1992.

KARE-TV, Minneapolis-St. Paul, October 21, 1991.

WCCO-TV, Minneapolis-St. Paul, October 2, 1991.

U.S. Merit Systems Protection Board. *Sexual Harassment in the Federal Government: An Update.* Washington, DC: U.S. Government Printing Office, 1980, 1988.

Warshaw, Robin. *I Never Called It Rape.* New York: Harper and Row, 1988.

DEVELOPING AND IMPLEMENTING SEXUAL HARASSMENT POLICY AND PROCEDURE

"If we can't turn to our parents and principals and they're not going to do anything for us, what's the point? That's what they're there for. They're supposed to help us learn and if we can't learn in an environment where we're being called names and stuff, then they're not doing their jobs."

—Female student

Has your administration developed and implemented a policy to prevent and reduce sexual harassment in your school and district? Is there a procedure in place for investigating sexual harassment, reporting incidents of sexual harassment, and giving consequences to harassers?

Some schools have developed a policy and procedure, but have not broadly disseminated it to students and staff. Many student handbooks do not inform students of their rights regarding sexual harassment, nor do they include information for students about what to do if they are sexually harassed.

One high school student handbook devoted a page and a half to rules of the library, and a third of a page to sexual harassment, including the school's definition of sexual harassment. The consequences for being caught smoking were more severe than the consequences for harassing a classmate.

The courts have ruled that an employer is held to a standard of absolute liability if he or she has implemented a sexual harassment policy but employees are either unaware that it exists or have no faith in its effectiveness. We can probably assume that the same would apply to a school with a sexual harassment policy that its students neither know about nor trust.

- When a sexual harassment policy exists and is widely disseminated, students, parents, administrators, and staff:

  - know that sexual harassment is illegal and will not be tolerated in the school

  - know what behaviors constitute sexual harassment

  - know the steps to follow if sexual harassment occurs

  - know the consequences to the harasser

  - know the rights and responsibilities of the individual to prevent sexual harassment from happening, and

  - know that there is confidential help and support available for the victim.

- Without a sexual harassment policy, students:

  - have no knowledge of their rights and responsibilities concerning sexual harassment

  - have no knowledge of what they can and should do about sexual harassment, and may

  - continue being harassed, or

  - continue harassing.

- Without a sexual harassment policy, parents:
  - lose confidence in the school as a safe and secure place for their children
  - start to see the school as a hostile and harmful environment for their children, and
  - if their children are the victims of sexual harassment, may take legal action against the school.

- Without a sexual harassment policy, administrators and staff:
  - have no knowledge of their rights and responsibilities
  - have no clear definition of sexual harassment
  - have no guidelines for dealing with harassers or harassing behaviors
  - are responsible for the negative consequences to the victim of sexual harassment, and therefore
  - risk potential liability.

A school without a sexual harassment policy and procedure is a school that supports sexual harassment. This support may be passive, covert, and subtle, but it is support nevertheless. When sexual harassment is present, inaction is a form of action.

GUIDELINES FOR DEVELOPING SEXUAL HARASSMENT POLICY AND PROCEDURE

To be in compliance with Title IX, every school district should have a sexual harassment policy and procedure that includes all or most of the elements described in this section. If your district already has a policy and procedure, you may want to check it against these guidelines. If your district does not have a policy and procedure, you may use these guidelines to develop and implement your own.

You may find it helpful to obtain copies of existing sexual harassment policies from other schools or districts, or workplace policies

from local companies. Because policies are constantly changing to reflect new laws and decisions regarding sexual harassment, and because they may vary from state to state, this curriculum does not include a sample policy, although it does include much information you will find useful when evaluating an existing policy or developing a new one.

If you can't locate an existing policy, or if you need further assistance developing and implementing a policy, contact your state Department of Education, Sex Equity Department; the Office of Civil Rights (Title IX); and/or your state's Human Rights Department. You should also plan to involve the attorney(s) for your school or district.

Your sexual harassment policy and procedure should include:

1. A philosophy statement regarding sexual harassment, emphasizing that it is illegal and will not be tolerated.

Try to keep it simple *and* legally correct —a real challenge! Do your best to put this philosophy (and the rest of the policy and procedure) in language that everyone can understand.

One Minnesota high school invited the students to help rewrite portions of its sexual harassment policy. This is a good way to get students involved and to make sure that the results are readable and comprehensible. Or you might ask students to put your policy in age-appropriate language for inclusion in the student handbook.

Example: "School district # (district number) is committed to providing a safe, positive learning and working environment for everyone. Therefore, we prohibit sexual harassment and sexual violence (SHV). We will not tolerate it in any form.

"It shall be a violation of this policy for any student or employee to use SHV toward any other student or employee. We will investigate all formal and informal, verbal and written complaints of SHV. Any student or employee who is found to have used SHV toward any other student or employee will be disciplined."

2. A definition of sexual harassment.

See page 5 for the EEOC's legal definition, along with several others.

You may want to add the following statement, after checking your state's sexual abuse statutes:

"Under certain circumstances, SHV may constitute sexual abuse under (name of state) statute (name of statute). In all such cases, we will comply with the statute and take immediate action to protect the victim(s) of the alleged abuse."

3. A list of specific behaviors that constitute sexual harassment.

See "Examples of Sexually Harassing Behaviors Reported in U.S. High Schools" on page 8 for a list you may want to use as a starting point. Precede your list with the statement, "Sexually harassing behaviors can include but are not limited to...." Avoid vague language and euphemisms.

4. Sanctions (consequences) for the student harasser.

Be specific, and spell out the consequences for a variety of behaviors.

If you choose to use progressive discipline —a system in which a first warning brings certain consequences, a second warning brings other (more severe) consequences, and so on—specify both the behaviors and the consequences. Be advised that progressive discipline should be used with extreme caution, if at all; obviously some harassing behaviors are more severe than others, and they merit a speedier and more severe response.

Consult with the attorney(s) for your school or district to make sure that sanctions fall within legal bounds.

Examples:

- a verbal warning/reprimand
- a written warning/reprimand, entered in the student's file
- suspension
- expulsion

- an apology to the victim
- a fine paid to the county sexual assault program
- writing a paper on the topic
- learning about sexual harassment (classes, reading, audio-visual programs, etc.)
- referral for psychological assessment
- a parent/student/school administration conference
- police involvement
- not being permitted to participate in extracurricular activities for a specific period of time
- community service
- other sanctions deemed appropriate by your school or district.

5. Sanctions (consequences) for the adult harasser (administrator, teacher, staff).

Consult with the attorney(s) for your school or district, and with the representative for your teachers' union, to make sure that sanctions fall within legal bounds.

Examples:

- a verbal warning/reprimand
- a written warning/reprimand, entered in the staff member's file
- suspension without pay
- termination of employment
- an apology to the victim
- a fine paid to the county sexual assault program
- learning about sexual harassment (classes, reading, audio-visual programs, etc.)
- referral for psychological assessment
- police involvement
- community service
- other sanctions deemed appropriate by your school or district.

6. **Sanctions (consequences) for the adult (administrator, teacher, staff) who is aware of sexual harassment but fails to act in accordance with school policy and procedure.**

School personnel need to report and/or investigate all incidents of SHV and take appropriate action, whether they personally observe these incidents or are made aware of them by some other means. Reporting, investigation, and action must occur even if the victim doesn't file a formal complaint, and even if the victim doesn't express any overt disapproval of the harassment. In the eyes of the law, teachers function as supervisors, which makes them legally liable for incidents of sexual harassment.

Examples: See #5 above.

7. **A student/staff code of conduct.**

A written code of conduct helps to maintain order and clarify the district's expectations of students and staff. Your code of conduct might include rules pertaining to the use of profanity, student behavior on school buses and during athletic events, smoking, cheating, food fights, the use of alcohol and other drugs, the school dress code, etc. It should also include a strong statement concerning sexually harassing and sexually violent behaviors.

8. **A statement of confidentiality.**

Example: "Information concerning any SHV complaint shall be treated confidentially and consistently with the district's legal obligations, the need to investigate, and the need to take disciplinary action if it is found that SHV has occurred."

9. **Options for informal resolution, when appropriate.**

Informal resolution can take the form of telling the harasser to stop the behavior and why. Or the victim may choose to write a letter to the harasser, a procedure described on pages 101–102. A sample letter is found on page 119.

10. **Names and titles of complaint manager(s).**

A complaint manager may also be identified as an investigator, Title IX coordinator, human rights officer, or simply a "resource person"; titles may vary from district to district.

Include both males and females. Ask your students to recommend people they trust and respect.

Examples: Title IX officer, Human Rights officer, student advocate, etc.

11. **A specific timeframe for responding to a complaint.**

Whether formal or informal, written or verbal, a complaint of SHV can be stressful for all concerned. This is one reason why all complaints should be investigated without delay. Also, the courts have ruled that complaints must be investigated in "a timely fashion." Although the precise meaning of "timely" may vary, in at least one case a wait of five days was judged to be too long.

Example: "Any person who believes that he or she has been a victim of SHV by a student or employee of this district shall report the conduct immediately to (name of resource person). Any third person with knowledge or belief of conduct which may constitute SHV shall report the conduct immediately to (name of resource person).

"If the report is made verbally, (name of resource person) shall document it in writing within 24 hours.

"An investigation shall begin immediately. Within ten days, the investigator(s) shall provide a written report of the status of the investigation to the alleged victim, the alleged perpetrator, and the superintendent."

12. **A procedure for disseminating the policy to students and staff.**

It's not enough to develop a sexual harassment policy. You must also make sure that students and staff know about it, have access to it, and understand what it means.

You should include the policy in the student/staff handbook; post it in the halls; give copies to new students and staff; include it in new student/staff orientation; present it in a special class on sexual harassment awareness and prevention; include it in all student and staff training regarding SHV; and present it to all students and staff in a school assembly.

13. **A statement dealing with reprisal and/or retaliation.**

Although some behaviors may not be legally defined as reprisal and/or retaliation, they may constitute abuse.* Keep this in mind when investigating complaints of SHV, and when developing policy and procedure.

Example: "Retaliation includes, but is not limited to, any form of intimidation, reprisal, or harassment.

"Anyone who retaliates against an individual who reports SHV will be disciplined. Anyone who retaliates against an individual who testifies, assists, or participates in an investigation, proceeding, or hearing relating to a complaint of SHV will be disciplined.

"Submission of a SHV complaint or report shall not affect that individual's employment, grades, work assignments, etc."

14. **A statement regarding students' rights and responsibilities.**

The activity on pages 104–105 invites students to brainstorm ideas about student rights and responsibilities. You may want to include your students' ideas in your policy and procedure.

Examples: "Every student has the right to a safe learning environment. Every student has the right to be treated with respect. Every student has the right to attend a school that is free of discrimination."

15. **A statement regarding the school's rights and responsibilities.**

The activity on pages 104–105 invites students to brainstorm ideas about school (and workplace) rights and responsibilities. You may want to include your students' ideas in your policy and procedure.

Examples: "Every school has the right and the responsibility to establish a code of conduct for students and staff. Every school has the right and the responsibility to develop and implement SHV policy, procedure, and programs. Every school is responsible for providing a safe learning and working environment for students and staff."

16. **A description of the investigative process.**

Investigating complaints of sexual harassment is a science and an art that takes real skill on the part of the investigator(s). That skill is best acquired through training. Various organizations provide such training, including your state Human Rights Department.

Example: "The investigation may consist of personal interviews with the alleged victim, the alleged perpetrator(s), and others who may have knowledge of the incidents or circumstances that led to the complaint. The investigation may also consist of other methods and documents specified by the investigator."

17. **A grievance procedure.**

A grievance procedure for incidents of sexual harassment is required by Title IX.

An incident should be reported first to the principal. If the victim is uncomfortable doing this—perhaps because the principal is the alleged perpetrator, or perhaps because the victim just doesn't want to go to the principal for whatever reason—then the incident should be reported to another administrator in the building or the district. Possibilities include the assistant principal, human rights officer, superintendent, or a school board member. Victims should be allowed (and in some cases encouraged) to bring along an advocate to offer support.

The victim should be prepared to report what happened, when it happened, where it happened, how she/he felt, what (if anything) she/he did or said in response to the harasser, what the alleged harasser(s) did or said next, and names of witnesses, if any. This information will be turned over to the individual(s) investigating the complaint.

---

*For example, a high school student in Minnesota was called a "liar" by school staff members after testifying before the Minnesota House of Representatives. Strictly speaking, this did not constitute reprisal and/or retaliation, but it was clearly abusive behavior.

A grievance procedure might include the use of a student advocate during the complaint/investigation process; a provision that allows informal resolution as an option (see #9 above); a provision that allows the victim some control over further institutional action;* a provision that allows the victim to participate in the decision-making process regarding the resolution, when appropriate; a description of the investigative process, with a timeframe (see #11 above); a statement about an appeal process; a statement regarding the titles and/or names of people involved in the investigation; and coordination with any other grievance procedure(s).

18. **A statement regarding appeals and alternative complaint procedures.**

If an alleged victim or perpetrator disagrees with the results of the investigation, she/he has the right to appeal and request another investigation. The victim also has the right, at any time, to pursue other options of recourse, including the State Department of Human Rights and/or civil action or redress under criminal statutes.

19. **A statement regarding training for staff and students.**

The *Sexual Harassment and Teens* curriculum is designed for use with students in grades 7 through 12. It can also be adapted for in-service training for staff.

Sexual harassment training can be integrated into existing curricula in social science, history, cultural awareness, and other subjects. Some schools have set aside one day each year for speakers and presentations dealing with SHV. Your statement should specify how often the training will be conducted.

Example: "All professional staff, other staff, and volunteers shall receive initial basic training about SHV. This training will cover the following topics:

- a definition of sexual harassment
- behaviors that constitute sexual harassment
- causes of sexual harassment
- contributing factors to sexual harassment
- the uses and abuses of power
- rights and responsibilities of the school and the student
- liability for sexual harassment
- a procedure to follow if one is a victim of sexual harassment
- a procedure to follow if one witnesses or otherwise becomes aware of sexual harassment
- the psychological effects on the victim
- the district's policy regarding sexual harassment
- confidentiality
- consequences to the harasser, and
- sexual harassment prevention.

"New employees shall receive training within the first two weeks of the school year. Each subsequent year, staff and volunteers will be required to attend additional training which will restate the district's commitment to provide students and staff with a harassment-free learning and working environment, and to provide staff with the opportunity to broaden their knowledge of related issues including male and female images in advertising, gender bias in the classroom, etc.

"Administrative employees who have specific responsibilities for complaints of SHV shall receive yearly training on investigating complaints, with emphasis on new laws and regulations.

"Students in grades K through 12 shall receive age-appropriate education in SHV. Depending on the age of the students, this education may cover the following topics:

- a definition of sexual harassment
- behaviors that constitute sexual harassment
- the causes of sexual harassment

---

*For example: A female student complains about a male student harassing her on the bus. She doesn't want to ride the bus with him anymore. The school decides that he can keep riding the bus, but she has to find other transportation, thereby re-victimizing her. This provision gives her some control over this decision.

- contributing factors to sexual harassment
- the district's policy and procedure regarding sexual harassment
- what to do if it happens to you
- how sexual harassment affects the victim, and
- consequences to the harasser.

"In addition, an age-appropriate curriculum will be adopted for use in the classroom to ensure that succeeding generations of students learn how to deal with SHV if it happens to them. This curriculum will also emphasize the importance of treating others with respect, so that the underlying causes of sexual harassment may be eliminated."

20. **A statement regarding the service personnel and services available to students and staff.**

    Personnel might include nurses, counselors, psychologists, and social workers who provide counseling and support to help individuals determine if they have been sexually harassed, cope with the effects of the harassment, and file complaints, when appropriate.

    Student services might include support groups for victims of SHV, and referrals to other agencies or organizations when appropriate.

    Student services may be provided within the education system, or in cooperation with other county agencies.

21. **A plan to involve students, staff, and community groups in the identification and prevention of sexual harassment and sexual violence.**

    Suggestions: Invite community groups such as the League of Women Voters, the Chamber of Commerce, and the Lions Clubs to play an active role in developing district policies, procedures, and programs relating to SHV. Inform parents about the policy and procedure via printed materials sent home with students. Include SHV-related issues in PTSA (Parent-Teacher-Student Association) programs and other public forums.

22. **A plan to communicate the policy, procedure, and programs to the community.**

    Suggestions: Post the policy on school bulletin boards, with the name of a contact person to call for more information (and make sure that person is accessible). Send home a brochure to parents and students. Include it in any and all of the following: adult education bulletins, community education bulletins, course handbooks, and student handbooks (written in age-appropriate language, preferably by the students themselves with staff assistance).

    Discuss the policy with all classes at the beginning of the year. Discuss it with all teachers before school begins and throughout the year. Announce it on TV and radio programs (perhaps through Public Service Announcements, or PSA's) and in the newspaper(s). Conduct special programs through community organizations, churches, and synagogues. Conduct parent workshops. Discuss SHV issues at parent-teacher conferences.

23. **A statement of intent to review and, if necessary, update sexual harassment policy, procedure, and programs on an annual basis.**

    Review the policy and procedure annually to determine whether they meet the newest legislative rulings. Form joint committees whose members are drawn from key community groups —the Chamber of Commerce, local churches or synagogues, human services, etc.—and work with them to develop policies for them to implement. Review all staff and student handbooks yearly, and revise them as necessary to reflect the latest version of your SHV policy and procedure.

Put the pieces together to help solve the puzzle of sexual harassment to teens in schools

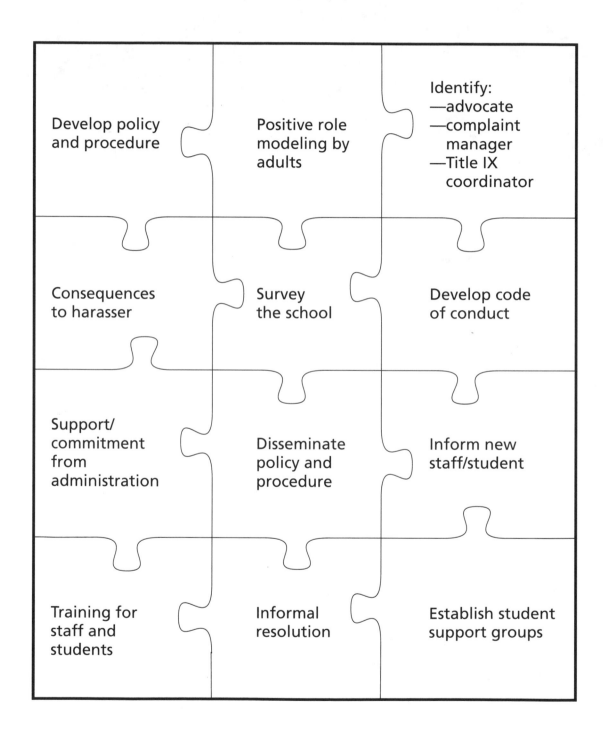

Develop policy and procedure

Positive role modeling by adults

Identify:
—advocate
—complaint manager
—Title IX coordinator

Consequences to harasser

Survey the school

Develop code of conduct

Support/ commitment from administration

Disseminate policy and procedure

Inform new staff/student

Training for staff and students

Informal resolution

Establish student support groups

25 WAYS TO PREVENT SEXUAL HARASSMENT

1. Train all staff—including teachers, administrators, aides, office staff, and maintenance personnel—in sexual harassment/violence awareness and prevention.

2. Train staff in gender bias awareness and prevention.

3. Offer equal numbers of sports to male and female students, with equal access to facilities, resources, and support.

4. Schedule speakers and offer classes in:

   • sexual harassment/violence awareness and prevention

   • sex role stereotypes

   • the role of the media (TV, movies, music, advertisements) in promoting violence and sex role stereotypes

   • healthy sexuality

   • healthy relationships

   • sexism in our culture and our language

   • women's contributions to American history, culture, etc.

   • conflict resolution

   • communication

   • assertiveness

   • choice making, decision making

   • stress management.

5. Offer student services to victims of sexual harassment, including referrals to agencies, psychologists, and special programs.

6. Involve parents and the community in your efforts to change attitudes and behaviors by:

   • forming a committee to keep the sexual harassment policy current, examine gender-fair curricula, and promote activities including speakers and plays, awards and scholarships based on equality issues or demonstrated respect for others

   • offering seminars on sexual harassment/violence awareness and prevention and related topics

   • discussing the issue at parent-teacher conferences

   • writing articles for local newspapers about what your school or district is doing about sexual harassment

   • sending information home to parents about sexual harassment policy and procedure.

7. Offer support groups to students involved in nontraditional classes and courses of study, and to female students and male students (separately).

8. If your state uses outcome-based education, develop learner outcomes that deal with sexual harassment and violence.

9. Encourage teachers and students to develop projects and units that promote the celebration of diversity.

10. Encourage school groups to sponsor various activities that increase sexual harassment/violence awareness. Examples: poster contests, writing contests, plays, presentations.

11. Preview all student skits prior to production. Work with the students to examine skits for signs of discrimination. Agree ahead of time on consequences for changes made subsequent to review, and follow through on those consequences. (Just as schools would not allow racial slurs in their student skits, they should not allow gender slurs.)

12. Check bathroom walls daily for inappropriate graffiti. Wash and/or paint the walls as needed.

13. Identify a student advocate to accompany victims who choose to file formal complaints.

14. Include the essentials of the sexual harassment policy in the student handbook, written in age-appropriate language; invite students to help you rewrite the policy for this purpose.

15. Offer recognition and/or awards to students and staff who serve as positive role models by treating people with dignity, respect, and equity.

16. Survey students and staff to learn the specifics about sexual harassment in your school. (Use the Sexual Harassment Survey on pages 134–138.)

17. Survey students and staff for suggestions on making the school environment safer, healthier, and more open for everyone.

18. Facilitate a peer helper program. (Students are trained in basic counseling techniques, then made available to kids who need to talk, but don't want to talk to adults.)

19. Train older students to teach younger students about sexual harassment/violence.

20. Encourage students to speak up if they are victimized by sexual harassment, or if they know of other students who are victimized.

21. Investigate and take appropriate action if you observe sexual harassment, or if you are made aware of it. Don't wait for victims to report the incidents or file formal complaints. Remember that many never do report or complain. Take a proactive position.

22. Use gender-inclusive language in all classes and activities.

23. Make use of the "teachable moment." For example, when an incident of sexual harassment occurs, take this opportunity to teach your class or school about sexual harassment and sexual violence, and to communicate that these behaviors are illegal and are not tolerated.

24. Develop a committee to tackle these issues and form a plan of action (including who, what, when, where, and how) to make the school environment healthy and harassment-free. If possible, include parents and community members.

25. A year following the implementation of your anti-harassment plan, evaluate your efforts and use the results to establish new goals and objectives for the next year.

GETTING READY TO TEACH THE PROGRAM

YOUR TEACHING STYLE

Any topic related to sex or sexuality has the potential to awaken strong personal feelings. Sexual harassment is an emotionally charged issue that may generate fear, anger, and confusion in teens and adults alike. Your teaching style will set the tone of the program in your classroom or group. It will affect your students' comfort level and willingness to confront the subject.

Before you begin the first unit, take time to assess your own attitudes and stereotypes. What are your beliefs about male and female roles, and how do your beliefs affect your behavior? What are your expectations of teens? What biases, if any, do you project based on a young person's gender, style of dress, background, or school performance? How comfortable are you with the topic of sexual harassment? Can you deal with it in an open, non-threatening, and non-threatened way?

Have *you* ever harassed anyone sexually? Could any of your behaviors that you interpret as innocent be construed as sexual harassment? Have you ever been sexually harassed? If so, how did you feel about it? How did you deal with it?

Most sexual harassment in junior/middle and senior high schools takes place in the classroom during class time. If you are a teacher, is it happening in your classroom? If it is, what are you doing about it?

These are tough questions, and you may not be able to answer all of them immediately.

But keep them in mind as you teach *Sexual Harassment and Teens*. They will affect the way you present the materials, and the way you respond to your students.

TEAM TEACHING THE PROGRAM

It is recommended that this curriculum be presented by a team of teachers, leaders, or facilitators—a male and a female. This increases the students' comfort level while providing positive male and female role modeling. It makes it safer for students of both genders to open up during the sessions, or afterward if they want to talk privately. Be sensitive to issues of multicultural diversity and ethnicity.

You may want to consider asking a school nurse, psychologist, social worker, counselor, or attorney to be your teaching partner, or to serve as a consultant or adviser to you during the program. This should be someone your students like, respect, and trust. Often, these professionals have expertise in the area of sexual harassment that could be useful and valuable to you. Don't forget them just because they aren't classroom teachers.

If it isn't possible for you to teach with another adult partner, rest assured that this program has been taught successfully by individuals like yourself. Besides, there's another group you can and should turn to for help: teens themselves.

TEENS AS TEACHERS

If you really want teens to sit up and take notice of this program, ask them to teach it with you!

This program is about sexual harassment and *teens*. Its primary focus is on the ways young people encounter sexual harassment—as victims, observers, and harassers—and what they can do about it. It does not assume that adults are the only experts in the room. In fact, the teens in your group may be more likely than you to have direct personal experience with sexual harassment on a daily basis. They may be the *real* experts.

When you invite teens to work beside you, sharing the power and the responsibility of teaching, you are sending a message that your group can't miss. You are letting them know that this isn't "just another class," with a teacher at the front teaching, and students at their desks listening—or not listening. You are making it clear that their input is valued and even essential to the success of the program.

You have much to gain from this inclusive approach. First, it's no secret that teens are more receptive to learning when they play an active role. You will probably find that the teens in your group respond with increased openness and trust when one of their leaders is "one of them." Seeing that you're willing to learn from them will make them more willing to learn from you. The program will become a group effort, with everyone working together to achieve the same goals.

Second, inviting students to help you teach will make your life easier. Teachers today are expected to take on much more than the three R's. State and federal mandates have placed much of the burden of solving society's problems on the schools. You may already be teaching teens about sex, alcohol and other drugs, and AIDS awareness and prevention. You may be counseling young people with family and/or personal problems. You may be offering courses on multicultural learning, diversity, and racism.

At least one state is considering a proposal to have schools teach violence prevention.

If your curriculum is overcrowded, *Sexual Harassment and Teens* may seem like an added burden. But by sharing it with your students, you'll find it a welcome addition. Their knowledge, insights, and energy may amaze you. You'll discover that it's a topic most of them want to know more about. Following are some suggestions to help get you started choosing student assistants:

- Look for teens who are sensitive, open-minded, and respected by their peers.

- Interview prospective teaching partners. Try to find out their feelings about sexual harassment. Have they had personal experience with it? Avoid teaming up with a female student who is angry at all males, or a male student who believes that females ask to be harassed.

- Consider asking three students to present the program with you—one for each unit. This spreads any "status" associated with teaching throughout the group, and it gives more students the chance to participate.

- Emphasize the time and commitment involved. Teen teachers will have to prepare for class and come to class on time.

- Give teen teachers the opportunity to preview the units and read the "Perspectives on Sexual Harassment" section (pages 3–22) before the program begins. If possible, each student assistant should have his or her own copy of this book.

- If you would prefer to have another adult as a teaching partner, you can still get teens involved. This program often calls for students to break up into smaller groups for activities or exercises. You can ask individual students to lead these groups, and to do any necessary reporting to the larger group when you reconvene.

For legal reasons, is it not recommended that this program be taught entirely by teens. There should always be at least one adult leader present.

REVIEWING THE PROGRAM MATERIALS

Be sure to review the individual units before starting to teach them. Familiarize yourself with the order in which the information is presented, check to see that the necessary resources and equipment are available, and be prepared for the student activities and discussions.

Try to get a feeling for whether the units will fit into the amount of time you have set aside for the program. The approximate time requirements indicated at the beginning of each unit are actually *minimum* time requirements, specified for the convenience of schools and organizations whose schedules are so tight that the only way to introduce new material is by squeezing it into a study hall or lunch period. *I encourage you to take as much time for this program as you possibly can.* Sexual harassment is a topic of growing importance to schools and organizations; please don't cut it short. Give yourself the opportunity to teach it thoroughly and comprehensively. Give your students the opportunity to ask questions, contribute to discussions, learn from one another, and do some serious thinking.

You'll notice that each unit includes several "suggested scripts." These are just as their name implies: *suggested.* Read through them carefully before you start teaching the program. Mark your notes and changes in the margins, where space has been provided for this purpose. Add your own thoughts, insights, and examples. Feel free to revise anything that doesn't fit for you.

For example, the first suggested script in Unit One begins, "For the next few days, we will be learning about sexual harassment...." As noted above, you may decide to take longer than that approximate (minimum!) time requirement. You may choose to devote a whole week (or longer) to this subject, making use of the supplemental activities and materials and developing new activities of your own. Or you may opt to present the program in a single all-day marathon session. Simply adapt the script accordingly.

The more you teach this program, the more personalized it will become, and the more it will reflect your teaching style and the specific needs of your students.

TEN TIPS FOR TEACHING THE PROGRAM

1. Approach the topic of sexual harassment in a non-blaming way. Take care to teach the facts (for example, "women are three times as likely as men to be victims of sexual harassment") without making judgments ("all men are sexual harassers"). This can sometimes be a difficult balance to maintain.

2. Read between the lines of what your students say in class. Sometimes what they don't say is more important than what they do say.

3. Praise your students, smile at them, and give them other kinds of validating messages to help them feel safe and secure in your classroom.

4. When dividing students into groups for activities and exercises, be sure to mix them to ensure diversity by gender, ethnic group, etc.

5. Use student feedback as cues for pacing the material. If your students seem to be getting increasingly uncomfortable, stop and talk about it. If they want to spend longer on a particular point than the curriculum indicates, try to accommodate them. You may find that you can complete some sections more quickly than you originally planned.

6. When appropriate, encourage disagreement. This shows that your students are thinking about the topic on a personal level.

7. When appropriate, use humor to make a point or lighten the mood. Humor facilitates learning and teaching.

8. If you have time, gather additional resources of your own before starting to teach the program. Look through newspapers and magazines for current cartoons, comic strips, articles, editorials,

letters, and more on the topic of sexual harassment. Use these to support the curriculum, add interest and immediacy, and, on occasion, for comic relief.

9. Remember that you are leading a class, not a therapy group. See "When Teens Need Extra Help" below.

10. Be prepared for almost anything! Especially for a course as emotionally charged and potentially volatile as this one, your students need to know that they can count on you.

Some students may react to the curriculum with resentment or disgust, while others may find their belief systems so challenged that they can't cope. They may question the validity of the unit and even defy you in class. Some students may be openly grateful that the topic is finally being addressed in public and in the safety of a classroom setting; others may experience intense discomfort as they see their own attitudes and behaviors reflected in the examples and case studies. Some students may get defensive or aggressive, acting out their anger and fear. Others may break down and cry. You will need to be there for them all.

WHEN TEENS NEED EXTRA HELP

Be alert for changes in your students' behavior. A sudden decline in school performance and/or attendance, fidgeting, withdrawal, moodiness, and acting out may indicate discomfort, anxiety, or defensiveness about the topic, or personal experience with sexual harassment or sexual abuse.

There may be students who come to you with their own stories of victimization. Respond with sensitivity and respect. Sometimes all a teen needs is someone to listen.

It may be necessary to refer troubled students to the school psychologist or social worker, or to an outside social service agency. Check with your principal or school psychologist to find out the proper way to make such referrals. Don't feel that you must try to solve everybody's problems on your own.

INTRODUCING THE PROGRAM

When introducing the program to your students, be sure to allow time for discussion of the many emotions the topic may elicit. Acknowledge that it will sometimes be difficult, embarrassing, and scary for everyone—including you—to talk about some of the issues that will be raised.

Remind your students of the need to disagree respectfully. It's okay to criticize a person's idea, but not to criticize the person. Tell them that humor, laughter, and jokes are allowed and encouraged as long as they are not at someone else's expense.

Ask your students what they need from you in order to feel safe in talking about sexual harassment. Work together to establish mutually agreed upon guidelines for class discussion. For example:

• Students have the right not to take part in any activity that seems threatening to them.

• Students are expected to respect each others' confidentiality. Anything of a personal nature that is discussed in the classroom stays in the classroom.

Let your students know that you will be available to talk with anyone who feels the need for individual time with you. For example, you might be available during a study hall or after school.

Depending on the amount of time you feel you need to adequately introduce the program to your students, you may want to consider introducing it the day before you begin teaching the first unit; see "Introduction" on pages 41–42. You will need Transparency #1, "Program Objectives" (page 54), and copies of "Definitions" (pages 59–60), one for each student.

PREPARING FOR THE FIRST UNIT

1. Review the resources and equipment list on page **40**.

2. Make transparencies #1–#5 (see pages **54–58**) or #2–#5, if you introduced the program earlier (transparency #1 is used in the introduction).

3. Make photocopies of "True or False?" (page **61**), one for each student.

4. Make photocopies of "Definitions" (pages **59–60**), one for each student, unless you introduced the program earlier ("Definitions" is handed out during the introduction).

5. Read through the Supplemental Activities on pages **51–53** and make any necessary preparations for those you plan to do.

WHAT IS SEXUAL HARASSMENT?

UNIT OBJECTIVES

1. To define sexual harassment

2. To identify sexually harassing behaviors

3. To clarify the differences between sexual harassment and flirting

4. To emphasize that people of both genders can be victims of sexual harassment

5. To introduce laws which prohibit sexual harassment

APPROXIMATE TIME REQUIRED

45–60 minutes

RESOURCES AND EQUIPMENT NEEDED

• Overhead projector and screen

• Transparencies #1–#5 (see pages **54–58**)

• Markers

• Flip chart/newsprint paper

• Copies of "Definitions" (pages **59–60**), one for each student

• Copies of "True or False?" (page **61**), one for each student

SUPPLEMENTAL ACTIVITIES

Unit One supplemental activities are found on pages **51–53**.

1. ORIENTATION

▸ Suggested script:*

(1) *For the next few days, we will be learning about sexual harassment. You may have heard that sexual harassment is a problem for adults in the workplace. It is also a problem for teenagers at school and at work. This course deals with the sexual harassment teenagers may experience.*

(2) *Sexual harassment isn't just a social problem. It can also be a legal problem. The United States Supreme Court has ruled that students who suffer sexual harassment and other forms of sexual discrimination can take legal action against their schools and school officials for violating their civil rights.*

(3) *Schools must be concerned with sexual harassment, and they must take steps to stop it from happening.*

(4) *Sexual harassment gets worse when it is ignored. We at (name of your school, district, or organization) have chosen not to ignore it. Instead, we're going to explore what it is. We're going to identify what causes it. And we're going to learn how to prevent it and stop it.*

(5) *By learning about sexual harassment, we will help to create a healthier school environment for everyone—students and staff.*

(6) *We will spend three class periods on this program, and we will approach this subject in many different ways. Some of the time will be spent on lectures, some will be spent in discussions, and some will be spent on small-group activities.*

(7) *When people talk about anything related to sex or sexuality, it can get embarrassing. This is true for adults as well as teenagers. As we talk about sexual harassment over the next few days, we may feel embarrassed sometimes. That's okay; it's part of being human.*

(8) *In this program, we agree to respect each others' feelings and privacy. You don't have to talk about anything you don't want to talk about. You don't have to answer questions you don't want to answer. You have the right to your own opinions.*

(9) *We also agree not to criticize one another or make fun of one another. We agree that we are here to learn.*

---

*Throughout this curriculum, the paragraphs in the suggested scripts are numbered to facilitate team teaching.

---

2. PROGRAM OBJECTIVES

- ▸ Show Transparency #1, "Program Objectives" (page **54**).

- ▸ Suggested script:

  (1) *These are the objectives of this class on sexual harassment—the things we will accomplish during the time we spend together.*

  (2) *We will define sexual harassment and identify behaviors which may constitute sexual harassment.*

  (3) *We will identify liability for instances of sexual harassment. This means that we will talk about the laws concerning sexual harassment, and the legal consequences of being a harasser.*

  (4) *We will describe the causes of sexual harassment.*

  (5) *We will identify the psychological effects of sexual harassment on the victim, the classroom or work unit, and the organization. Sexual harassment hurts everyone.*

  (6) *We will consider the financial consequences of sexual harassment to the victim and the organization.*

  (7) *We will learn the proper procedure to follow if sexual harassment occurs.*

  (8) *Who has questions or comments about what I've said so far? Remember that this is just an introduction to the program. We will discuss each of the objectives in more detail later on.*

- ▸ Allow a few moments for questions and discussion before concluding the introduction to the program.

- ▸ End by passing out copies of "Definitions" (pages **59–60**), one to each student. Tell the class that this handout will help them to understand some of the important words and language used in the program. Encourage them to bring "Definitions" to every session.

II. DEFINING SEXUAL HARASSMENT AND IDENTIFYING SEXUALLY HARASSING BEHAVIORS

1. EXAMPLES OF SEXUAL DISCRIMINATION

- ▸ Suggested script:

  (1) *Sexual harassment is a type of sexual discrimination. Sexual discrimination happens when someone is treated differently than other people because of his or her gender.*

▸ If necessary, explain the meaning of the word "gender" (one's sex—male or female).

> (2) *For example, women usually make less money than men for doing the same or equivalent work. Mothers rather than fathers usually get custody of their children after a divorce.*

> (3) *What are some other examples of sexual discrimination?*

▸ Allow a few moments for students to offer their examples and ideas.*

2. DEFINITION OF SEXUAL HARASSMENT

▸ Suggested script:

> (1) *Sexual harassment is illegal in the schools according to Civil Rights Act Title IX of the Federal Education Amendments. It is illegal in the workplace according to Civil Rights Title VII. These are federal laws that apply to everyone in the United States.*

> (2) *Some states make sexual harassment illegal through their State Departments of Human Rights.*

> (3) *Here is a general definition of sexual harassment, according to the Equal Employment Opportunities Commission, an agency of the United States Government.*

▸ Show Transparency #2, "Definition of Sexual Harassment" (page 55).

▸ Read the definition aloud to the students. Provide a simplified translation for younger students, or if any students appear to have difficulty understanding any part of the EEOC definition.

▸ If necessary, explain the meaning of the following terms:
- "sexual advances" (coming on to someone; trying to lure someone into a sexual act)
- "sexual favors" (sexual acts performed in return for a reward, such as a promotion or a higher grade)
- "verbal conduct of a sexual nature" (inappropriate and unwanted comments about a person's body, clothing, gender, etc.)
- "physical conduct of a sexual nature" (inappropriate and unwanted touch).

---

*There will be many times during this program when you ask students for examples. You may want to record their examples for future reference, or for use in future Sexual Harassment classes. One teacher suggests putting individual examples on 3" x 5" cards and filing them by category in a small file box. You will build up quite a collection for times when students get stuck, or when you need ideas for student activities.

---

3. STUDENT ACTIVITY: SEXUALLY HARASSING BEHAVIORS VS. FLIRTING BEHAVIORS

- ▶ Divide the class into two groups, A and B. Give flip chart paper and markers to each group.

- ▶ Instruct the students in Group A to work together to list as many sexually harassing behaviors as they can remember having seen or heard about at school or at work. Tell them that these behaviors may have occurred on the bus, during a football game, in the locker room, during lunch, in the halls, in the parking lot, in the classroom, etc. See page 8 for a list of examples.

- ▶ Instruct the students in Group B to brainstorm a list of behaviors they think of as flirting, and to write their list on flip chart paper.

- ▶ Tell them not to judge the behaviors. For example, one student may say "winking," and another may respond "that's not flirting, that's sexual harassment." Remind the students to stick to the basic rules of brainstorming:

    RULE #1: Everybody tries to come up with as many ideas as possible.

    RULE #2: All ideas are acceptable during brainstorming.

    RULE #3: It's okay to piggyback on other people's ideas.

    RULE #4: Nobody judges or criticizes anybody else's ideas.

- ▶ Allow a few moments for the groups to compile their lists.

- ▶ Post the lists on the wall for all to see.* Bring the groups back together again. Have a spokesperson from each group read their list aloud.

III. IDENTIFYING THE SIMILARITIES AND CLARIFYING THE DIFFERENCES BETWEEN SEXUAL HARASSMENT AND FLIRTING

1. IDENTIFYING THE SIMILARITIES

- ▶ Discuss with the class the similarities between the items on the two lists, Sexually Harassing Behaviors and Flirting Behaviors.

2. CLARIFYING THE DIFFERENCES

- ▶ Suggested script:

    (1) *What, in your opinion, is the major difference between sexual harassment and flirting?* (Flirting feels good to both parties involved. Sexual harassment doesn't feel good to the person who is being harassed.)

---

*You may want to retain these lists and others generated during this program for future reference, or for use in future Sexual Harassment classes.

SEXUAL HARASSMENT AND TEENS

(2) *Is it possible for someone to start off by flirting with another person, and it somehow turns into sexual harassment?* (Yes.)

(3) *How do you think this happens?* (The person being flirted with pretends to go along with it when she/he really doesn't like it. Or the person being flirted with doesn't mind it at first, but stops feeling good about it, and the other person keeps doing it anyway.)

(4) *What matters is how the person on the receiving end perceives the behavior, not how the person doing the behavior wants it to be perceived. The law protects the victim. It's the victim's perception that counts.*

▸ The following paragraph is key to understanding sexual harassment. Present it to your class *slowly* and *carefully*. Repeat if necessary.

(5) *The law is concerned with the impact of the behavior, not the intent of the behavior. In other words, the law is concerned with how the person on the receiving end is affected by the behavior, not with what the other person means by the behavior. This is a VERY important concept. Does everyone understand it? Who can give an example?*

▸ Allow a few moments for questions, clarification, and examples. You may need to further simplify or expand on this concept.

▸ Suggested script:

(6) *Most of us wouldn't want to do or say something if we knew it would hurt another person. We know that it's important to respect other people's feelings, just as we want them to respect our feelings.*

(7) *Although the law protects the victim, it's up to us as individuals to take responsibility for the things we say and do.*

3. STUDENT ACTIVITY: FEELINGS

▸ Divide the class into two groups, A and B. Give flip chart paper and markers to each group.

▸ Instruct the students in Group A to write a list of feelings that a victim of sexual harassment would experience following the incident. (For examples, see pages **14** and **16**.)

▸ Instruct the students in Group B to write a list of feelings that an individual would experience while being flirted with. (For examples, see page **16**.)

▸ Allow a few moments for the students to compile their lists.

▸ Post both lists on the wall for all to see. Bring the groups back together again. Have a spokesperson from each group read their list aloud.

4. IN THE EYE OF THE BEHOLDER

▸ Suggested script:

> (1) *While there are many similarities between sexual harassment and flirting, there is one big difference: how the person on the receiving end feels as a result of the behavior.*

> (2) *Part of this has to do with power. Flirting usually relates to sexual attraction—a strong feeling, but not an abuse of power. Sexual harassment happens when one person uses his or her power in an abusive way.*

> (3) *Sometimes it's hard to know when a particular behavior is flirting and when it is sexual harassment. Often, as the saying goes, it's "in the eye of the beholder."*

▸ Show Transparency #3, "In the Eye of the Beholder" (page 56).

▸ Discuss with the students the meaning of the phrase "in the eye of the beholder." Be sure that they understand what the terms "victim," "harasser," and "perception" mean. Re-emphasize that the victim's perception is what matters in cases of sexual harassment, not the harasser's intent—even if the intent was to flirt or compliment.

5. COMPLIMENT OR HARASSMENT?

▸ Suggested script:

> (1) *Imagine this scene: Jill comes to school wearing a new sweater. Jack tells Jill, "Hey, you look great in that sweater today." Jill takes it as a compliment. Is this sexual harassment?* (No.)

> (2) *Now imagine this scene: Jack tells Jill, "Hey, you look great in that sweater today." Something about the way he says it—or the way she hears it—makes Jill feel angry, embarrassed, and maybe even guilty. Is this sexual harassment?* (Yes.)

> (3) *Sometimes it's hard to know if something you say or do will be taken in a different way than you intend it. You may worry about that when you're thinking about giving someone a compliment. Everyone in this class may worry about it sometimes. We don't want other people—especially our friends—to feel angry, embarrassed, or guilty because of something we say or do.*

> (4) *It's important to understand that it's not only WHAT you say, but HOW you say it that counts. Your tone of voice, the look on your face, and your body language all add up to send different kinds of messages.*

> (5) *If Jack looks at Jill like a friend, smiles at her like a friend, and says, "Hey, you look great in that sweater today" in a friendly, normal voice, he is sending one kind of message.*

(6) *But if Jack rolls his eyes or winks, leers at Jill, makes rude gestures with his hands or his body, and says, "He-e-e-ey....you look GREAT in that SWEATER today," he is sending another kind of message.*

(7) *Here are three general guidelines to keep in mind at times like these:*

(8) *First, don't say or do anything you wouldn't want to see printed in the newspaper or broadcast on TV.*

(9) *Second, don't say or do anything you wouldn't want your parents, sister or brother, girlfriend or boyfriend to find out about.*

(10) *And third, don't say or do anything you wouldn't want the other person's parents, sister or brother, girlfriend or boyfriend to find out about.*

(11) *In other words, if you wouldn't say something to a girl in front of her boyfriend, don't say it when her boyfriend isn't around.*

IV. BOTH GENDERS CAN BE VICTIMS

▸ Suggested script:

(1) *Do you think that only girls can be sexually harassed? Or can boys be harassed, too?* (Yes, boys can be sexually harassed.)

(2) *Who do you think sexually harasses boys?* (Girls and other boys.)

(3) *About 15 to 30 percent of men in the workplace state that they have been sexually harassed. To date, no studies have been done to find out how many boys in schools have been sexually harassed. Do you think many are?*

▸ Allow a few moments for discussion. Invite students to give examples of sexual harassment directed at boys.

▸ Suggested script:

(4) *Studies show that males and females perceive sexual attention in different ways, and that men and boys tend to like getting sexual attention from women and girls. They are often flattered by it and perceive it as a compliment.*

(5) *Most sexual harassment occurs to women and girls by men and boys. Females are three times as likely to be harassed as males. Because sexual harassment is more common with females, most of the examples we discuss in this program will have women and girls as the victims.*

1. SEXUAL HARASSMENT IS ILLEGAL WHEN...

▸ Show Transparency #2, "Definition of Sexual Harassment" (page 55) again. Review the definition. Remind the students that this definition is from the Equal Employment Opportunity Commission—the EEOC, an agency of the United States Government. Explain that it is a legal definition.

▸ Show Transparency #4, "Sexual Harassment Is Illegal When..." (page 57).

▸ Suggested script:

> *This definition is also from the EEOC. Let's go over it one point at a time.*

2. ...IT IS A TERM OR CONDITION OF EMPLOYMENT

▸ Suggested script:

> (1) *Sexual harassment is illegal when, number 1, "Submission to such conduct is made either explicitly or implicitly a term or condition of an individual's employment." What does this mean?* (That an employer cannot hire you or fire you based on whether you go along or don't go along with his or her sexual attentions. When you "submit" to something, you don't do it willingly or eagerly; you do it reluctantly—it's not something you want to do, and it's not something that makes you feel good.)

▸ If necessary, explain the meanings of "explicit" (clearly and precisely stated or expressed; straightforward, direct) and "implicit" (understood, but not directly stated or expressed; implied or hinted at).

▸ Give examples. (Explicit: "To get this job, you'll have to have sex with me." Implicit: "To get this job, you'll have to stay late once or twice, if you know what I mean.") Provide further information for younger students, or if any students appear to have difficulty understanding any part of the definition.

▸ Suggested script:

> (2) *If this ever happens to you at work—if an employer hires you or fires you based on whether you go along with his or her sexual attentions— it is your right to file a formal complaint and/or take legal action.*

> (3) *This kind of sexual harassment can also happen at school. It just looks different. For example, a coach or adviser may approach you sexually, saying or implying that you have to go along if you want to make the hockey team or the debate squad. This is illegal. If this ever happens to you, it is your right to file a formal complaint and/or take legal action.*

3. ...IT AFFECTS EMPLOYMENT DECISIONS

▸ Suggested script:

> (1) *Sexual harassment is illegal when, number 2, "submission to or rejection of such conduct by an individual is used as the basis for employment decisions affecting such individual." What does this mean?* (That an employer can't decide to give you—or not to give you—a raise or a promotion based on whether you go along or don't go along with his or her sexual attentions.)

> (2) *If this ever happens to you at work—if an employer gives you or doesn't give you a raise or a promotion based on whether you go along with his or her sexual attentions—it is your right to take legal action.*

> (3) *At school, it is illegal if a teacher says or implies that you won't fail a course, or you will get an "A," if you go along. It is illegal if a coach promises that you will be captain of the team, or an adviser says that you will be president of the student council, if you give in to the sexual pressure.*

> (4) *Even if the consequences are only implied—even if your coach doesn't come right out and say that you'll be captain—it is still sexual harassment if you feel pressured sexually.*

> (5) *Both number 1 and number 2 deal with situations where people have power over you. At work, this usually means your boss. At school, it can mean a teacher, a coach, or any adult who is in a position of authority.*

> (6) *Who has questions about this part of the definition?*

▸ Allow a few moments for questions and discussion.

4. ...IT INTERFERES WITH WORK PERFORMANCE OR CREATES A HOSTILE ENVIRONMENT

▸ Suggested script:

> (1) *Sexual harassment is illegal when, number 3, "such conduct has the purpose or effect of unreasonably interfering with an individual's work performance or creating an intimidating, hostile or offensive working environment." What does this mean?*

▸ Allow ideas and questions; clarify if necessary.

▸ Suggested script:

> (2) *Number 3 is the most common type of sexual harassment in the schools. And it doesn't only come from people in positions of authority.*

(3) *A harasser can be another student who is bigger than you, or has more social status. It can be your chemistry lab partner, the person whose locker is next to yours, or someone you see in the halls between classes.*

(4) *What happens when sexual harassment interferes with your school work? What happens when it creates an environment that feels intimidating, hostile, or offensive to you? You stop wanting to come to school. You are sick and tired of being harassed. Or maybe you are scared.*

(5) *You don't have to put up with being sexually harassed. You have options and choices. We will look at these later on, in Unit Three.*

VI. ENDING THE UNIT

▶ Show Transparency #5, "Mother Goose & Grimm" (page 58).

▶ Suggested script:

(1) *Sometimes it helps to laugh about serious things. Anytime you can think of a way to lighten up this class, please do! If you find cartoons or comic strips that fit with the things we're learning about, bring them in and we'll pass them around.*

(2) *Before we end this session, who has a question or something to say?*

▶ Allow a few moments for questions and discussion.

▶ Summarize the curriculum for this unit (or review the Unit Objectives on page 40) and tell the class the topic of the next unit: "What Are the Causes of Sexual Harassment?"

▶ End by passing out copies of "True or False?" (page 61), one for each student. Instruct the students to complete the exercise before the next unit and bring it to class with them. Tell them that this will be the opening activity for Unit Two.

PREPARING FOR THE NEXT UNIT

1. Review the resources and equipment list on page **64**.

2. Make transparencies #6–#19 (see pages **81–94**).

3. Find out if your school or district currently has a sexual harassment policy and procedure. You will need this information for Part III, "How Sexual Stereotypes, Myths, and Assumptions Support Sexual Harassment" (pages **66–71**).

4. Read through the Supplemental Activities on pages **78–80** and make any necessary preparations for those you plan to do.

QUESTIONS FOR DISCUSSION

1. Is sexual harassment a conscious behavior, an unconscious behavior, or both? Explain. (*It can be either or both. Some people may consciously choose to harass others on purpose. Others may do it as a result of their upbringing or conditioning; that's just the way they treat people.*)

2. Is there any difference between boys harassing girls and girls harassing boys? Explain. (*No. Harassment is harassment regardless of gender.*)

3. What are the legal rules about sexual harassment? What are the social rules about sexual harassment for most people your age? How do the two compare? (*Legal rules state that sexual harassment is illegal; social rules may excuse, allow, or condone sexual harassment.*)

4. Is there any connection between sexist language and sexual harassment? Explain. (*Sexist language can be a form of sexual harassment.*)

5. Can students sexually harass teachers? Have you seen or heard of this happening in your school? Give examples. (*Yes, students can harass teachers.*)

6. Do you think it's possible for harassers not to know how their victims perceive their behavior? Do you think it's possible for victims to perceive flirting as sexual harassment? If you perceive another person's behavior as sexual harassment, does that mean it is sexual harassment? (*When there's a question about intent vs. impact, it's the impact that counts.*)

7. Maybe it's okay for your best friend to touch you under your chin or tickle you under your arms. Would it be okay for everyone to touch you in those places? Why or why not? (*Certain parts of our bodies are off limits to some people but not to others. Certain parts are off limits to everybody.*)

8. What are some other factors that can determine if it's okay for someone to touch you? (*Who the person is; your relationship with him or her; whether he or she has power over you; the time and place; etc.*)

ROLE REVERSAL

Have students assume the role of the opposite sex in conversation, flirting, and sexually harassing behaviors. Follow up with discussion on how it feels to be perceived and treated as a member of the opposite sex. Ask students if they think their feelings and perceptions are accurate. Why or why not?

CURRENT EVENTS

Obtain magazine or newspaper articles about sexual harassment cases. Have students read the articles and report on the cases to the rest of the class. Tell them to be sure to include any legal principles they found in the articles. (To review the legal principles, see Transparency #4, "Sexual Harassment Is Illegal When...," page 57.)

PROFESSIONAL OPINION

Invite an attorney, human rights officer, sex equity specialist, Title IX coordinator, or another expert on sexual harassment/discrimination to visit your class to talk about sexual harassment and answer students' questions.

LOADED LANGUAGE

Divide the chalkboard in half. Label one half "MEN/BOYS" and the other half "WOMEN/GIRLS." Further divide each half into four columns labeled "food," "plant," "animal," and "other." The board should look like this:

MEN/BOYS				WOMEN/GIRLS			
Food	Plant	Animal	Other	Food	Plant	Animal	Other

SEXUAL HARASSMENT AND TEENS

Divide the class into groups. Instruct each group to brainstorm names and words in each category that men/boys and women/girls are called. Have them write their names and words on the board. Anything goes!

Examples:

- For "food": Honey, sugar
- For "plant": Rose, weed
- For "animal": Fox, chick, dog, cow, kitten
- For "other": Babe, hunk, male, female

Ask the students to label each word "negative" or "positive," or to give each one a minus sign or a plus sign. Ask them if there are any words that are neutral, and to label neutral words with a 0.

Count the number of positive and negative names/words for each sex. Which sex has more negative names/words? Which sex has more positive names/words?

Bring to the students' attention various words that are often used as compliments (examples: "fox" and "chick") but are actually demeaning and sexist. Discuss how these words relate to sexual harassment, disrespect for the opposite sex, and the tendency to perceive other people as sex objects.

PROGRAM OBJECTIVES

☑ To define sexual harassment and identify behaviors which may constitute harassment.

☑ To identify liability for instances of sexual harassment.

☑ To describe the causes of sexual harassment.

☑ To identify the psychological effects of sexual harassment on the victim, the classroom or work unit, and the organization.

☑ To consider the financial consequences of sexual harassment to the victim and the organization.

☑ To learn the proper procedure to follow if sexual harassment occurs.

DEFINITION OF
SEXUAL HARASSMENT

Any unwelcome sexual advances, requests for sexual favors, and other verbal or physical conduct of a sexual nature....

(EEOC)

IN THE EYE OF THE BEHOLDER

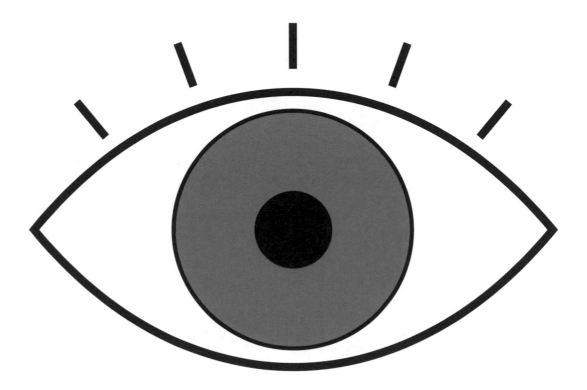

SEXUAL HARASSMENT IS ILLEGAL WHEN...

1. Submission to such conduct is made either explicitly or implicitly a term or condition of an individual's employment.

2. Submission to or rejection of such conduct by an individual is used as the basis for employment decisions affecting such individual.

3. Such conduct has the purpose or effect of unreasonably interfering with an individual's work performance or creating an intimidating, hostile or offensive work environment.

(EEOC)

MOTHER GOOSE & GRIMM

Reprinted by permission of Tribune Media Services.

DEFINITIONS

Assumption (noun) Something that is taken for granted; something that is accepted as true, even if there is no real proof
  Assume (verb)

Coerce (verb) To use force, threats, or intimidation to make a person act a certain way
  Coercion (noun)
  Coercive (adjective)

Discrimination (noun) Treating someone differently because of his/her gender, race, religion, disability, etc.; not treating the person as an individual; prejudice
  Discriminate (verb)

Employee (noun) Someone who works for another person or company (an **employer**) for pay

Explicit (adjective) Clear, direct, straightforward

Exploit (verb) To use someone or something unfairly, for your own purposes, profit, or advantage
  Exploitation (noun)
  Exploitative (adjective)

Gender (noun) One's sex, male or female

Harass (verb) To annoy, intimidate, frighten, threaten, or bully another person
  Harasser (noun)
  Harassment (noun)

Implicit (adjective) Not clear, direct, or straightforward; implied or hinted at

Intent (noun) A person's reason for saying or doing something

Legal (adjective) Having to do with the law

Liability (noun) Legal responsibility, legal obligation
  Liable (adjective)

Myth (noun) A popular belief, story, or tradition that is used to explain something

Perceive (verb) To become aware of through your senses
  Perception (noun)

Physical sexual conduct (noun) Touching another person in a sexual way, usually to show affection; in the case of sexual harassment or sexual violence, this touch is inappropriate and unwanted

Reject (verb) To refuse someone or something
  Rejection (noun)

Respect (noun) A special feeling of high regard for someone or something; esteem, consideration, courtesy
  Respect (verb)
  Respectful (adjective)

Sex object (noun) Someone who is seen only as an object of sexual interest, not as a person

Sex role stereotyping (noun) Expecting men and women to be and act a certain way because of their gender ☞

Sexism (noun) Discrimination or prejudice based on gender; stereotyping people by gender
   Sexist (adjective)

Sexual advances (noun) Come-ons; attempts to lure someone into a sexual act

Sexual discrimination (noun) Discrimination based on gender

Sexual favors (noun) Sexual acts performed in return for a reward, such as a promotion or a higher grade

Sexual harassment (noun) Unwelcome sexual advances, requests for sexual favors, and other verbal or physical conduct of a sexual nature

Sexual violence (noun) Sexual acts meant to hurt or harm another person physically and emotionally; rape is an act of sexual violence

Stereotype (noun) A mental picture that people in one group have of people in another group; a stereotype assumes that people will have certain abilities, characteristics, behaviors, and values just because they belong to a certain race, gender, religion, social class, family, etc.

Submit (verb) To go along with something because you have to, not because you want to
   Submission (noun)

Verbal sexual conduct (noun) Sexual comments about a person's body, clothing, gender, etc.; in the case of sexual harassment or sexual violence, these comments are inappropriate and unwanted

Victim (noun) A person who is injured or otherwise harmed by the actions of another; someone who is oppressed, mistreated, or tricked
   Victimize (verb)

TRUE OR FALSE?

Read each statement.

Circle "T" for TRUE if you think the statement is *generally* or *usually* true.

Circle "F" for FALSE if you think the statement is *generally* or *usually* false.

T   F   1. Sexual harassment is a problem in the workplace.

T   F   2. Sexual harassment is a problem in the schools.

T   F   3. Men/boys can be victims of sexual harassment.

T   F   4. If a woman/girl dresses or behaves in a sexy way, she is asking to be sexually harassed.

T   F   5. Sexual harassment can occur between people of the same sex.

T   F   6. Women in professional jobs (teachers, lawyers, engineers, doctors, etc.) are not as likely to be sexually harassed as women in blue-collar jobs (factory workers, secretaries, truck drivers, etc.).

T   F   7. Women/girls rarely file false charges of sexual harassment.

T   F   8. Saying "NO" is usually enough to stop sexual harassment.

T   F   9. If sexual harassment occurs in the school between students, it is illegal and the school is responsible.

T   F   10. Women/girls who work in jobs that are usually held by men (construction workers, accountants, surgeons, etc.) are more likely to be sexually harassed.

T   F   11. Most women/girls enjoy getting sexual attention at work and at school.

T   F   12. Most men/boys enjoy getting sexual attention at work and at school.

T   F   13. The only people who can harass women/girls at work/school are those in positions of authority (employers, teachers, administrators).

T   F   14. Women/girls use their sex appeal to get what they want at work and at school.

T   F   15. One of the best ways to deal with sexual harassment is to ignore it.

T   F   16. Women of color are sexually harassed more often than white women.

T   F   17. Most victims of sexual harassment report it to their employer or school principal.

T   F   18. If *he* didn't like the sexual attention, but *she* meant it only as flirting or joking, then it was not sexual harassment.

T   F   19. Teasing and flirting are no big deal. They make school and work more fun.

T   F   20. Schools/workplaces should know if sexual harassment is occurring among their students/employees.

WHAT ARE THE CAUSES OF SEXUAL HARASSMENT?

1. To examine facts and opinions about sexual harassment

2. To identify the causes of sexual harassment

3. To determine how sexual stereotypes, myths, and assumptions support sexual harassment

4. To examine two studies on sexual harassment

APPROXIMATE TIME REQUIRED

45–60 minutes

RESOURCES AND EQUIPMENT NEEDED

• Overhead projector and screen

• Transparencies #6–#19 (see pages **81–94**)

• Markers

• Flip chart/newsprint paper

• Completed "True or False?" handouts from Unit One

SUPPLEMENTAL ACTIVITIES

Unit Two supplemental activities are found on pages **78–80**.

I. TRUE OR FALSE?

- Collect the completed handouts.

- Randomly pass them back to the students, making sure that each student receives another student's completed paper.

- For each question, start by asking students to indicate which answer appears on the paper they have. (Example: "For Question 1, how many of you have 'TRUE' circled? Raise your hands.") Then give the correct answer to the question, with the explanation. The answer key is on pages 75–77.

II. CAUSES OF SEXUAL HARASSMENT

1. SEXUAL HARASSMENT EQUATION

- Show Transparency #6, "Sexual Harassment Equation" (page 81).

- Ask the students what it means. (If there was equality between men and women, there would be no sexual harassment.) Allow a few moments for ideas and discussion.

- Suggested script:

  (1) *In many countries around the world, women are perceived as second-class citizens. They are simply not seen as being very important. They have very few rights. They can't own property. In some countries, women are property—they belong to their fathers before they are married, and to their husbands after they are married.*

  (2) *Let's talk for a few moments about the status of women in our country.* Women aren't usually considered property, and they do have rights. But are they still second-class citizens? What are your opinions about this? Give examples.*

- Allow a few moments for students to offer their opinions and examples.

- Show Transparency #7, "Sally Forth" (page 82). Read the comic strip aloud. Invite the students to comment on it. (One point they—or you—should be sure to make is that women's contributions are not considered important enough to include in our education.)

---

*There is ample data available on how the media, government, the educational system, etc. treat females as inferior to males. If you and your students are interested, consider creating your own unit around this fascinating topic.

---

2. THE ABUSE OF POWER

- ► Show Transparency #8, "The Abuse of Power" (page 83).

- ► Suggested script:

    (1) *Imagine a continuum of sexual violence, with rape and murder at the far end. Sexual harassment is on that continuum, too. Often, it is not motivated by sexual attraction, but by anger. The harasser uses sex as a way of expressing that anger and taking it out on somebody else.*

    (2) *In our society, gender means power—or the lack of power. Our government, churches, businesses, courts, and schools are run by men. Women still earn only 70 cents for every dollar men earn. Men hold the power.*

    (3) *Some things are changing, and some women are assuming more powerful positions. But there is still an imbalance of power in our culture.*

    (4) *To some people, power is exciting and even sexy. They use their power to embarrass, intimidate, and control other people.*

    (5) *There are two kinds of power you should know about. One kind is formal power—the kind given to people in positions of authority. Employers, principals, and teachers have formal power.*

    (6) *Another kind is informal power—the kind given to males by our culture. Some men assume this informal power and use it to verbally and physically harass other people, especially women.*

    (7) *Women who don't go along with the harassment are labeled "unfriendly" or "cold." They are accused of not being able to take a joke. It is said that there is "something wrong with them."*

    (8) *Who has an example of a time when you felt harassed (angry, embarrassed, guilty), and the other person tried to blame it on you?*

- ► Allow a few moments for examples.

III. HOW SEXUAL STEREOTYPES, MYTHS, AND ASSUMPTIONS SUPPORT SEXUAL HARASSMENT

1. CONTRIBUTING FACTORS IN SEXUAL HARASSMENT

- ► Show Transparency #9, "Contributing Factors in Sexual Harassment" (page 84).

- ▸ Suggested script:

> *Why is sexual harassment a problem in our society? Why does it keep happening, even when many people agree that it should stop? There are eight main reasons. Let's go over them one at a time.*

2. SOCIAL NORMS ENCOURAGE IT

- ▸ Suggested script:

> (1) *Sexual harassment keeps happening because our social norms encourage it. Our society pushes adults and teens to be sexual. Sex is used to sell everything from cars to toothpaste. Advertising exploits women by dressing them in bikinis or short, tight clothes and photographing them in suggestive poses. We are seeing more men being exploited, too.*

- ▸ If necessary, explain the meaning of the word "exploit" (to unfairly use someone or something for your own purposes and advantage).

> (2) *Movies and TV programs often show sex scenes which portray women as sex objects. What does the term "sex object" mean?* (A person who is regarded exclusively as an object of sexual interest, not as a person.)

> (3) *Sometimes it's difficult for males to understand what females feel when they are routinely portrayed as sex objects. Males do not perceive sexual attention as negatively as females do. They may even enjoy it.*

- ▸ Show Transparency #10, "Beetle Bailey" (page 85). Read the comic strip aloud. Invite students to comment on it. Ask them how this difference in perception can contribute to sexual harassment. (Males may believe that because they enjoy sexual attention, females enjoy it, too. When females don't enjoy it, but men keep giving it, this is the point at which sexual attention becomes sexual harassment. Remind the students that harassment is in the eye of the beholder. It is always a matter of impact, not intent.)

- ▸ Suggested script:

> (4) *A study was done in California about how men and women felt about being propositioned at work—about being asked if they wanted to have sex. Sixty-seven percent of the men were flattered. Only 17 percent of the women were flattered.*

- ▸ Return to Transparency #9, "Contributing Factors in Sexual Harassment" (page 84).

- ▸ Suggested script:

> (5) *Let's mention some other ways in which our social norms encourage sexual harassment.*

(6) *Many movies—especially movies aimed at teens—connect sex and violence. Women are usually the victims.*

(7) *The same goes for much of the music we hear today—especially music aimed at teens. The lyrics set women up as sex objects to be used for pleasure. If women say "no," or if they talk back, have their own opinions, or don't go along, the lyrics tell about forcing them, hurting them, or even killing them. Music videos show women almost exclusively as sex objects.*

(8) *Advertising sends the message that it's okay to use women to sell products. We see this every day on television; on packaging for products, including album covers; in magazine and newspaper ads; and on billboards. We hear it on the radio.*

(9) *Teens tend to model their behavior on adult behavior. What you see and hear in movies, TV programs, music, and music videos influences your perceptions, attitudes, and behavior.*

3. LACK OF CLEAR COMMUNICATION

▸ Suggested script:

(1) *Sexual harassment keeps happening because people don't communicate very clearly.*

(2) *For example, a woman says "no," but she says it nicely, and she smiles when she says it. Maybe she is smiling because she is embarrassed, or because she doesn't want to seem rude. Maybe she doesn't want to show her anger.*

(3) *Even if a woman says "no" without smiling, men may not believe that she means it. Boys are taught that when girls say "no," they are just playing games or pretending, and they really mean "maybe" or "yes."*

(4) *Meanwhile, girls are taught to put other people's feelings first. They don't want to hurt boys' feelings, so they aren't honest about their own feelings.*

(5) *When we hear what we want to hear, and say what we think other people want to hear, no wonder everyone feels confused!*

4. SEX ROLE STEREOTYPING

▸ Ask the students what the word "stereotype" means. (A stereotype is a standardized mental picture held in common by members of a group. It is usually based on an oversimplified opinion or uncritical judgment. It assumes that an individual or group will have certain abilities, characteristics, behaviors, and values just because he or she belongs to a certain race, gender, religion, social class, family, etc. Racism stereotypes people by race; sexism stereotypes people by gender.)

▶ Allow a few moments for students to offer definitions. Make sure that everyone understands this concept before continuing.

▶ Divide the class into two groups, A and B. Give flip chart paper and markers to each group.

▶ Suggested script:

> (1) *Sex role stereotyping means that we expect men and women to be and act a certain way, just because of their gender.*

> (2) *Let's explore the stereotypes of the "ideal high school girl" and the "ideal high school boy."*

▶ Instruct the students in Group A to list as many words and phrases as they can that describe the "ideal high school girl." (Examples: thin, sexy, no zits, pretty, passive, likes attention from boys, etc.)

▶ Instruct the students in Group B to do the same for the "ideal high school boy." (Examples: strong, doesn't cry, athlete, handsome, always wants sex, etc.)

▶ Allow a few moments for the students to compile their lists.

▶ Post the two lists on the wall for all to see. Bring the groups back together again. Have a spokesperson from each group read their list aloud.

▶ Suggested script:

> (3) *Take a look at these two lists. Compare them in your mind. Do you know anyone who actually fits these descriptions? Would you really like to know anyone who fits these descriptions?*

> (4) *Stereotypes ignore the fact that we are all unique, individual human beings. Sex role stereotyping is one reason why sexual harassment keeps happening.*

> (5) *Stereotypes aren't true, but we act as if they are. Sometimes we use them to make fun of people. For example, if a girl doesn't laugh at a sexist joke, we call her a "prude" or "too dumb to get it." Boys who show their feelings are labeled "queers" or "fags" or "homos." This type of name-calling is in itself a form of sexual harassment.*

> (6) *Teens who try to challenge these stereotypes don't get much support from their peers, society, and sometimes their own parents. Girls are told that boys won't like them if they show their intelligence. Boys are told that they are "wimps" if they don't fit the stereotype of the tough-guy "macho" male.*

5. ADULT ATTITUDES

▸ Suggested script:

> (1) *Sexual harassment keeps happening because many adults excuse it. They excuse it in themselves, which is obvious from the many cases of sexual harassment in the workplace.*

> (2) *They also excuse it in teens. They say, "Oh, that's just normal teenage behavior," or "This is how kids learn their limits," or "Boys will be boys," or "They're only girls—what do you expect?"*

> (3) *Actually, the phrase "boys will be boys" is used to excuse all kinds of behavior—not just sexual harassment—that would not be excused for girls. Our society has a double standard when it comes to male and female behavior. The same rules don't apply to both.*

▸ Show Transparency #11, "The Family Circus" (page 86). Read the comic aloud. Invite the students to comment on it.

▸ Suggested script:

> (4) *What are some other phrases you have heard that reflect adult attitudes about sexual harassment?*

▸ Allow a few moments for examples and discussion.

6. LACK OF SEXUAL HARASSMENT POLICY, PROCEDURE, AND TRAINING

▸ Return to Transparency #9, "Contributing Factors in Sexual Harassment" (page 84).

▸ Suggested script:

> (1) *Does our (school, district, organization) have a sexual harassment policy?*

▸ Allow a few moments for responses and discussion. If your students don't know the answer to this question, tell them the answer. If your school or district does have a sexual harassment policy, you may want to summarize it briefly. If your school or district doesn't have a sexual harassment policy, you may want to share any information you have about this issue. For example, is a policy being developed? Is this program a step in that direction?

▸ Suggested script:

> (2) *Do you know what to do if you are sexually harassed in school?*

> (3) *Do you know who to go to and tell if this happens to you?*

- Allow a few moments for responses and discussion. If your students don't know the answers to these questions, tell them the answers. Of course, your answers will depend on whether your school or district has a procedure in place. If it does, you may want to summarize it briefly. If it doesn't, you may want to offer suggestions. For example, should a student who is sexually harassed go to the school principal? To the school counselor? To a teacher?

- Suggested script:

> (4) *You are receiving training about sexual harassment right now, in this program. Do you think that school staff should receive training, too? Why or why not?*

- Allow a few moments for responses and discussion.

- Suggested script:

> (5) *How many of you have jobs?*

> (6) *Do you know if your workplace has a sexual harassment policy?*

> (7) *Have you ever received any training at work about sexual harassment?*

- Allow a few moments for responses to these questions.

> (8) *Without a clear policy and procedure, and without training, sexual harassment keeps happening. It isn't enough to have a policy if people aren't trained in what it means, why it exists, and how to enforce it. It isn't enough to have training if there isn't a policy to support it. Policy, procedure, and training are all needed—together—in order to stop and prevent sexual harassment.*

7. LACK OF FOLLOW-THROUGH; NO CONSEQUENCES TO HARASSER; THE VICTIM DOESN'T REPORT IT

- Suggested script:

> (1) *Without sexual harassment policy and procedure—and sometimes in spite of policy and procedure—many incidents of sexual harassment are never followed through. Nothing happens after the harassment occurs.*

> (2) *Often, there are no consequences for harassers. They are not held accountable for their actions, so they don't take responsibility for them. They keep harassing, and nothing changes.*

> (3) *Meanwhile, most victims of sexual harassment never report it. Fewer than five percent of sexual harassment incidents in the workplace are ever reported.*

> (4) *What percentage do you think gets reported in our school?*

- Allow a few moments for responses and discussion.

1. ILLINOIS TASK FORCE

▶ Show Transparency #12, "Illinois Task Force on Sexual Harassment in the Workplace Survey" (page 87). Read it aloud to the students. Invite students to comment on the results of the survey.

▶ If necessary, explain the meaning of the word "coercive" (to coerce someone is to force him or her to do something by pressure, threats, or intimidation).

2. SEXUAL HARASSMENT OF TEENAGE FEMALES

▶ Show Transparency #13, "Sexual Harassment of Teenage Females" (page 88).

▶ Suggested script:

(1) *In 1986, 250 teenagers from four Minnesota school districts were surveyed to find out how much sexual harassment they were experiencing at work and at school.*

(2) *Fifty percent of the girls said that they were being sexually harassed at school. Another 30 percent said that they were being harassed at work. That brought the total to 80 percent of the girls who said they were experiencing sexual harassment. Only three of the boys said they had been harassed.*

▶ Show Transparency #14, "Who Did the Harassing?" (page 89).

▶ Suggested script:

(3) *Most of the harassment occurred among students. About one-third of the girls said that they had been harassed by teachers. Nine percent said that they had been harassed by school administrators. The two percent marked "other" includes the school janitor, secretary, cook, and so on.*

(4) *If we surveyed the students in our school—if we asked how many were being harassed, and who their harassers were—what do you think the results would be?*

▶ Allow a few moments for student responses.

▶ Show Transparency #15, "What Type of Sexual Harassment Did You Experience?" (page 90).

▶ Suggested script:

(5) *The girls in the survey were asked what type of sexual harassment they experienced. Seventy-three percent said "remarks"—things that were said to them. Fifty-nine percent said "staring."*

(6) *Fifty-nine percent said "touch." It's important to realize that when sexual harassment involves unwanted touching, it crosses over into sexual assault. Sexual assault is a crime.*

(7) *Fifty-two percent said "gestures," seven percent said "propositions," and nine percent said "other."*

(8) *Most of the girls had been sexually harassed in more than one way.*

▶ Show Transparency #16, "When Did the Harassment Occur?" (page **91**).

▶ Suggested script:

(9) *The girls in the survey were asked to tell when they were harassed. You can see from the chart that most of the harassment went on during class or between classes. Do you think this would be true for our school?*

▶ Allow a few moments for responses.

▶ Show Transparency #17, "Where Did the Harassment Occur?" (page **92**).

▶ Suggested script:

(10) *The girls in the survey were asked to describe where they were harassed. You can see from the chart that it usually happened in class or in the hallways, between classes—the same results shown on the previous chart.*

▶ Show Transparency #18, "What Did You Do about the Harassment?" (page **93**).

▶ Suggested script:

(11) *What did the girls do about the harassment they were experiencing in class, in the hallways, from other students, from teachers—almost everywhere in school, from almost everyone? Most of them just ignored it.*

(12) *This is the way most people respond to sexual harassment—including students in school and adults in the workplace.*

(13) *Ignoring sexual harassment is the worst thing to do about it.*

▶ Show Transparency #19, "Who Did You Talk to about the Harassment?" (page **94**).

▶ Suggested script:

(14) *The girls in the survey ignored the harassment, but they did talk about it. Most of them told their friends. About one-third of them told their parents. Notice that not very many of them told a teacher or school administrator.*

(15) *The "agency" category refers to sexual assault organizations, mental health clinics, and so on. The "other" category refers to members of the clergy or health professionals.*

(16) *Why would a friend be the most likely person to talk to about being sexually harassed? Why would teachers and school administrators be among the least likely people to talk to?*

▸ Allow a few moments for responses and discussion.

V. ENDING THE UNIT

▸ Summarize the curriculum for this unit (or review the Unit Objectives on page **64**) and tell the group the topic of the next unit: "How Can We Prevent and Stop Sexual Harassment?"

PREPARING FOR THE NEXT UNIT

1. Review the resources and equipment list on page **96**.

2. Prepare a set of "Assumptions and Attitudes" notecards for use in the first student activity (page **97**). Write the following statements on individual notecards:

   - "She asked for it"
   - "She can't take a joke"
   - "She enjoys it"
   - "All boys want is sex"
   - "The way she dresses says she wants it"
   - "Boys will be boys"
   - "It's only flirting"
   - "Everyone else does it"
   - "Let them have their fun"
   - "She's a troublemaker"

   Ask your teen teacher(s) for additional ideas or alternate ideas more appropriate to your school or group.

3. Make transparencies #20–#22 (see pages **115–117**).

4. Obtain a copy of your school or district's sexual harassment policy and procedure. If none is available, try to borrow one from another school or district, or bring in a workplace policy and procedure. Thoroughly familiarize yourself with the policy. Make photocopies, one for each student.

   NOTE: No sample policy has been included in this curriculum because policies are constantly changing to reflect new laws and decisions regarding sexual harassment, and also because policies may vary from state to state and district to district. If you need help locating a policy to review with your students, contact your state Department of Education, Sex Equity Department, or the Office of Civil Rights (Title IX)/Human Rights Department.

5. Make photocopies of the following, one for each student:

   - "What to Do If It Happens to You" (page **118**)
   - "Sample Informal Resolution Letter" (page **119**)
   - "Sexual Harassment Survey" (pages **134–138**)
   - "Course Evaluation" (pages **139–140**).

6. Make photocopies of the following, one of each:

   - Case Studies: Secondary Schools (pages **120–126**)
   - Case Studies: Workplaces (pages **127–132**).

1. **Sexual harassment is a problem in the workplace.**

   TRUE. Studies show that 75–90 percent of working women have experienced sexual harassment. (See question #3 below for information about men in the workplace.)

2. **Sexual harassment is a problem in the schools.**

   TRUE. In one study, 50 percent of teenage girls reported that they had been sexually harassed at school. Many articles have been published about the problem of sexual harassment for women in colleges and vocational-technical schools. (Currently there is no hard data available about sexual harassment and teenage boys, although we do know that it happens.)

3. **Men/boys can be victims of sexual harassment.**

   TRUE. About 15–30 percent of men say that they have been sexually harassed in the workplace. Men in nontraditional jobs may experience more sexual harassment than men in traditional jobs. It is not known what percentage of boys in secondary schools are victims of sexual harassment.

4. **If a woman/girl dresses or behaves in a sexy way, she is asking to be sexually harassed.**

   FALSE. This is blaming the victim. Dressing or behaving in a sexually provocative way doesn't cause sexual harassment, although it may increase the likelihood that one will become a victim. On the other hand, NOT dressing or behaving in a sexually provocative way doesn't PREVENT harassment. The underlying problem is the way society teaches girls and boys to relate to each other. Girls are taught that winning the approval of boys and men is all-important, and that the best way to do it is by looking sexy; boys are taught that being sexually aggressive is "macho" and "cool," and that when girls dress in a sexy way, they are asking for sexual attention.

5. **Sexual harassment can occur between people of the same sex.**

   TRUE. This is more common among males than among females. It is estimated that male-to-male sexual harassment accounts for 20 percent of all male sexual harassment complaints. Three percent of sexual harassment complaints by women involve female-to-female harassment. The law doesn't differentiate between opposite-sex harassment or same-sex harassment; it applies to both kinds.

6. **Women in professional jobs (teachers, lawyers, engineers, doctors, etc.) are not as likely to be sexually harassed as women in blue-collar jobs (factory workers, secretaries, truck drivers, etc.).**

   FALSE. It is believed that professional women and blue-collar women experience the same amount of sexual harassment. Professional women *may* experience more subtle forms of sexual harassment, while harassment directed toward blue-collar women *may* be more overt.

7. **Women/girls rarely file false charges of sexual harassment.**

   TRUE. False charges are believed to account for less than 2 percent of the total. Most women refuse to report sexual harassment when it does occur due to lack of support, fear, self-blame, embarrassment, and other factors. It seems extremely unlikely that they would go through all the trouble and pain of reporting sexual harassment if it did not actually occur.

8. **Saying "NO" is usually enough to stop sexual harassment.**

   FALSE. Most sexual harassment is motivated by power. Therefore, a "no" may have no effect. Some teens report that saying "no" has actually increased the sexual harassment. Also, it is very difficult for a victim to say "no" to an employer, teacher, coach, or even to a popular peer. Those people have power.

9. **If sexual harassment occurs in the school between students, it is illegal and the school is responsible.**

   TRUE. Sexual harassment is illegal according to Title IX, whether it occurs between a teacher and a student or between two students. The school is definitely responsible if the harassment is occurring in the school or during school activities. The school, the principal, teachers, and other school staff may be held liable for the illegal harassment. This means that they can be held personally responsible for the harassment, and charged under civil law.

10. **Women/girls who work in jobs that are usually held by men (construction workers, accountants, surgeons, etc.) are more likely to be sexually harassed.**

    TRUE. Women in nontraditional jobs tend to be victims of sexual harassment more often than women in traditional jobs. The reasons are unclear, but it is believed that power plays a role. A woman in a non-traditional job is usually in the minority and is therefore more vulnerable. This is also true for men/boys who work in jobs that are usually held by women (such as nursing).

11. **Most women/girls enjoy getting sexual attention at work and at school.**

    FALSE. Most women/girls are angry, annoyed, and embarrassed by sexual attention at work and at school. They report feeling negated and belittled when their sexuality is noticed instead of their personhood, professional attributes, and intelligence.

12. **Most men/boys enjoy getting sexual attention at work and at school.**

    TRUE OR FALSE. This is a tough one. Some groups of males report that they *do* enjoy it, while others report that they *do not* enjoy it. Men *do not* enjoy being sexually harassed. (Remember that harassment is *unwanted* sexual attention.) However, many men indicate that they are flattered by some sexual attention. Their perceptions of what constitutes unwanted sexual attention may differ from women's perceptions.

13. **The only people who can harass women/girls at work/school are those in positions of authority (employers, teachers, administrators).**

    FALSE. Customers, coworkers, classmates, and friends can also be harassers.

14. **Women/girls use their sex appeal to get what they want at work and at school.**

   FALSE. The belief that women/girls use their sex appeal inappropriately is largely a myth. Most women want to be recognized and rewarded for their work/school performance and professional/scholarly expertise, not for being sexy.

15. **One of the best ways to deal with sexual harassment is to ignore it.**

   FALSE. Sexual harassment escalates when it is ignored. Victims must take action to stop the harassment. They must report it to authorities.

16. **Women of color are sexually harassed more often than white women.**

   TRUE. Women of color tend to be victimized in many ways. Because they are often in the minority, they are more vulnerable. They may be in low-level, low-paying jobs, where people in power can abuse their power. Various cultural myths perpetuate the idea that women of color enjoy or expect constant sexual attention.

17. **Most victims of sexual harassment report it to their employer or school principal.**

   FALSE. It is estimated that less than 5 percent of sexual harassment incidents in the workplace are reported. How many do you think are reported in schools?

18. **If *he* didn't like the sexual attention, but *she* meant it only as flirting or joking, then it was not sexual harassment.**

   FALSE. If a person perceives sexual attention as sexual harassment, then it *is* sexual harassment. Remember that the law is concerned with the *impact* of the behavior, not the *intent* behind it. Sometimes the intent is genuinely innocent, and a behavior is misunderstood as harassment. In most of these cases, the behavior stops when the victim explains how he/she feels about it. Often, people don't understand how sexist remarks or behaviors can affect others.

19. **Teasing and flirting are no big deal. They make school and work more fun.**

   FALSE. Remember that sexual harassment is in the eye of the beholder. What may be teasing to one person may be sexual harassment to another.

20. **Schools/workplaces should know if sexual harassment is occurring among their students/employees.**

   TRUE. They are responsible for providing an environment that is free of sexual discrimination and harassment. The courts say that an organization is liable for sexual harassment that occurs among employees and/or students, and that employers should know if it is occurring. Teachers/managers should be able to read cues from students and staff that harassment may be occurring.

QUESTIONS FOR DISCUSSION

1. What are some of the ways boys respond when a girl says "no"?

2. Does the way a person dresses affect the kind of attention she/he gets? Do you think that if a woman/girl or a boy/man dresses sexy, she or he should get sexual attention? Explain.

3. How do sexual stereotypes affect your own relationships with persons of the opposite gender?

4. Is there a way to NOT be pressured to fit sex role stereotypes? How easy is it for teenagers to be different from these stereotypes?

5. How do these stereotypes limit peoples' choices about how to act or dress?

6. How do these stereotypes affect teens in general?

7. Why do you think students who are sexually harassed don't feel comfortable talking about it, especially to teachers and school administrators?

8. Do boys/men get the message that they have a right to harass girls/women? Where does that message come from?

9. What are some reasons why a girl/woman might harass a boy/man?

10. What do you think might happen if a boy tried to stop other boys from sexually harassing someone?

11. What does the word "respect" mean? What does it mean to treat another person with respect?

12. What parts make up a whole person? *(Body, intellect, emotions, values, relationships, social skills, spirituality, etc.)* When one person is sexually harassing another, what part of the victim is getting the attention? What parts are being ignored and disregarded?

OFFENSIVE ADVERTISING

Ask students to bring to class examples of magazine and newspaper ads or TV commercials that exploit women and/or men. What products are the ads promoting? Discuss the message of each ad.

Encourage the students to write letters to the companies whose products are being promoted, explaining that they find the ads offensive and that they will boycott the products until they see evidence of better advertising. Tell them to request replies from the advertisers.

MACHO MAN

Show a picture of a "macho man" to the class. (You'll find plenty of examples in magazine advertisements.) Tell them to write a story about him—his thoughts and feelings, his views about women, his views about himself and his role in the world, and so on.

Do the same with a picture of a seductive-looking woman.

IDEALS AND MESSAGES

Ask the students to watch TV programs and commercials and evaluate them for the following messages:

- What is the ideal male? the ideal female?

- What are the costs—personal and financial—of being an ideal?

- How do males and females relate to each other?

- In the typical TV/commercial relationship, who is in control? Who *appears* to be in control? Who is responsible for maintaining the relationship?

- In the typical TV/commercial relationship, which gender advertises which types of products? (Examples: Men and beer; women and household cleaners.) What does this say about cultural stereotypes and gender roles?

Encourage the students to write letters to the networks and advertisers whose programs and commercials they find offensive. Tell them to request replies. Following are the addresses for the three major networks:

ABC	CBS	NBC
47 West 66th Street	51 West 52nd Street	30 Rockefeller Plaza
New York, NY 10023	New York, NY 10019	New York, NY 10112

PLAYING FAVORITES

Ask the students to pick a favorite athlete, rock star, movie star, or other role model/famous person. Tell them to identify what these people tell society about sex, sexuality, and stereotypes.

ANYTHING YOU CAN DO...

Divide the class into two groups—males and females. Give them the following assignments:

- Have the males list 5 things females can do but males can't.

- Have the females list 5 things males can do but females can't.

- Have each group list the advantages of being a member of their gender.

- Have each group list the disadvantages of being a member of their gender.

- Compare and discuss the lists.

MASCULINE OR FEMININE?

Ask students to brainstorm words that are used to describe people. Write their words on the flip chart. (If necessary, give them a few examples to get them started: honest, brave, pretty, sensitive, helpful, etc.)

Next, tell them to think about each word and decide if it usually describes a male or a female. Mark each word with an "M" or an "F" depending on how they respond. When opinion is divided, take a vote; the majority wins.

Use discussion to tie this activity into sex role stereotyping.

• Ask the girls how many of the qualities labeled "M" they see in themselves.

• Ask the boys how many of the qualities labeled "F" they see in themselves.

• Are they comfortable having qualities that are traditionally assigned to people of the opposite gender?

• Do they think it is healthy or unhealthy to have qualities of both genders?

SONGS AND LYRICS

Ask students to bring in tapes and lyrics of popular songs. Play the songs, read the lyrics, and discuss the message of each song. Discuss with the students how the message might affect teen attitudes and behaviors.

FAMILY TRADITIONS

Ask students to interview their parents and grandparents about the roles of men and women when they were growing up. Discuss their findings.

• What were the attitudes each gender had about the other?

• How have those attitudes changed—if they have changed?

Ask individual students how their attitude compares with their parents' attitude. Ask how it compares with their grandparents' attitude.

SEXUAL HARASSMENT EQUATION

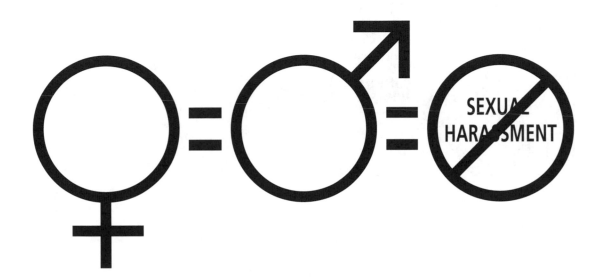

SALLY FORTH

Sally Forth / By Greg Howard

Reprinted with special permission of
North America Syndicate, Inc.

THE ABUSE OF POWER

CONTRIBUTING FACTORS IN SEXUAL HARASSMENT

- Social norms encourage it

- Lack of clear communication

- Sex role stereotyping

- Adult attitudes

- Lack of sexual harassment policy, procedure, and training

- Lack of follow-through

- No consequences to harasser

- The victim doesn't report it

BEETLE BAILEY

Reprinted with special permission of
King Features Syndicate, Inc.

THE FAMILY CIRCUS

"You say 'boys will be boys' when Billy and Jeffy do something. How 'bout 'girls will be girls'?"

Reprinted with special permission of King Features Syndicate, Inc.

ILLINOIS TASK FORCE ON SEXUAL HARASSMENT IN THE WORKPLACE SURVEY

- 1500 women responded

- 70% said they had been sexually harassed

- Type of sexually harassing behavior experienced:

  - Sexual remarks/teasing 52%

  - Looks/leers 41%

  - Subtle sexual hints/pressure 26%

  - Touched/grabbed 25%

  - Propositioned 20%

  - Repeatedly pressured for sex 14%

  - Coercive sex 2%

  - Other 9%

Source: Illinois Task Force on Sexual Harassment and Sangamon State University. *Task Force Survey Reported to Illinois House Judiciary Committee, March 4, 1980.* Springfield: Sangamon State University, 1980.

SEXUAL HARASSMENT
OF TEENAGE FEMALES

50% sexually harassed at school

30% sexually harassed at work

TOTAL: 80% sexually harassed

Source: NASSP Bulletin

WHO DID THE HARASSING?

Teacher 30%

Administrator 9%

Other 2%

Student 59%

Source: NASSP Bulletin

WHAT TYPE OF SEXUAL HARASSMENT DID YOU EXPERIENCE?

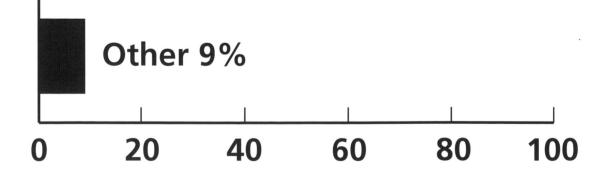

Remarks 73%

Staring 59%

Touch 59%

Gestures 52%

Propositions 7%

Other 9%

| 0 | 20 | 40 | 60 | 80 | 100 |

Source: NASSP Bulletin

WHEN DID THE HARASSMENT OCCUR?

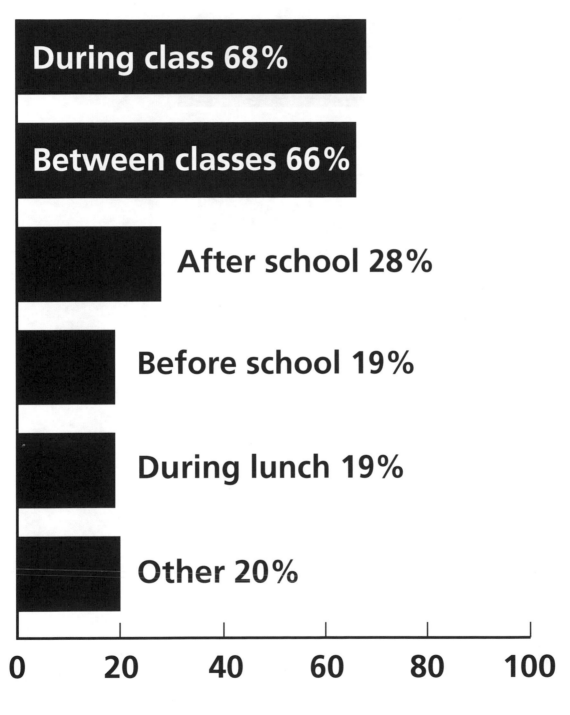

During class 68%

Between classes 66%

After school 28%

Before school 19%

During lunch 19%

Other 20%

Source: NASSP Bulletin

WHERE DID THE HARASSMENT OCCUR?

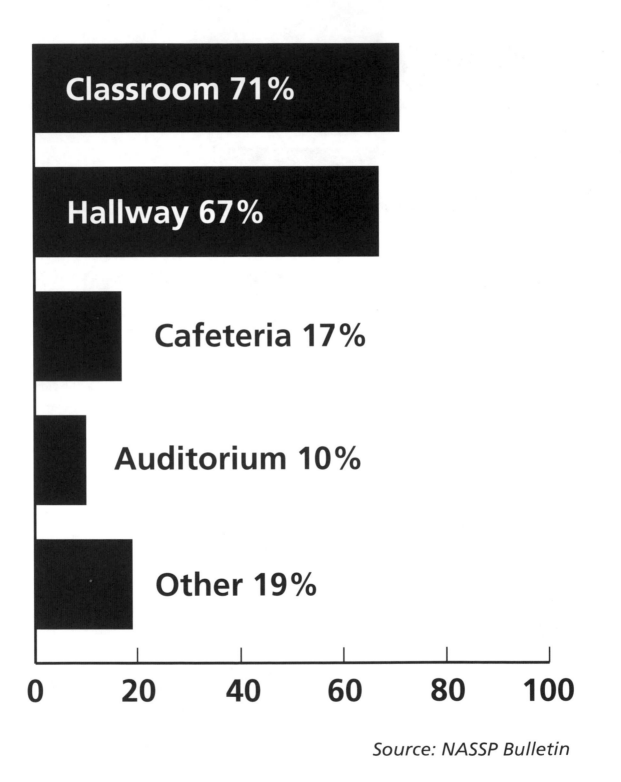

Classroom 71%

Hallway 67%

Cafeteria 17%

Auditorium 10%

Other 19%

0   20   40   60   80   100

Source: NASSP Bulletin

WHAT DID YOU DO
ABOUT THE HARASSMENT?

Ignored it 69%

Hit harasser 14%

Changed classes 6%

Reported it to principal 6%

Talked to harasser 6%

Talked to teacher or counselor 2%

Missed school 1%

Other 10%

| 0 | 20 | 40 | 60 | 80 | 100 |

Source: NASSP Bulletin

WHO DID YOU TALK TO ABOUT THE HARASSMENT?

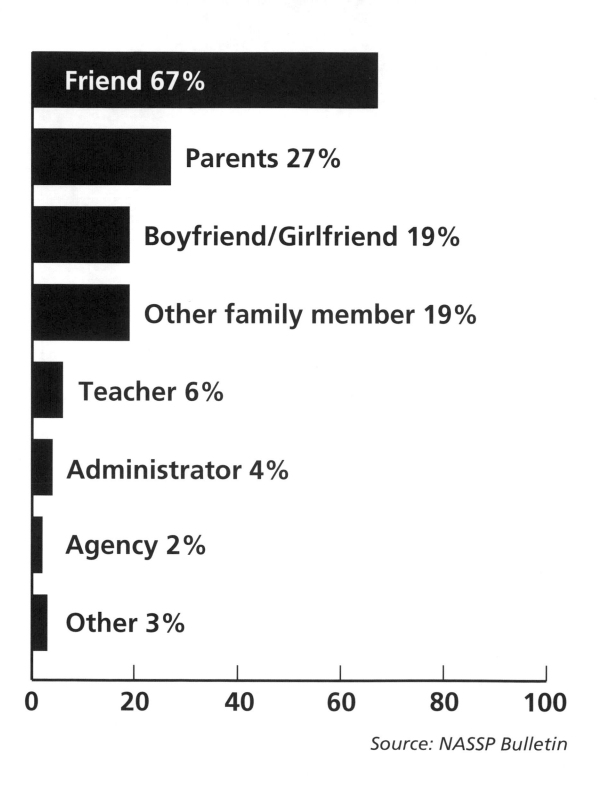

Friend 67%

Parents 27%

Boyfriend/Girlfriend 19%

Other family member 19%

Teacher 6%

Administrator 4%

Agency 2%

Other 3%

| 0 | 20 | 40 | 60 | 80 | 100 |

Source: NASSP Bulletin

HOW CAN WE PREVENT AND STOP SEXUAL HARASSMENT?

UNIT OBJECTIVES

1. To explore how sexual harassment affects the victim and the organization

2. To examine your school or district's sexual harassment policy

3. To explain how to report incidents of sexual harassment

4. To consider sexual harassment case studies

5. To review student and school rights and responsibilities concerning sexual harassment

6. To gather information about sexual harassment in your school

APPROXIMATE TIME REQUIRED

45–60 minutes

RESOURCES AND EQUIPMENT NEEDED

- "Assumptions and Attitudes" note cards (see page **74**)

- Overhead projector and screen

- Transparencies #20–#22 (see pages **115–117**)

- Pencils or pens

- Markers

- Flip chart/newsprint paper

- Copies of your school or district's sexual harassment policy, or another policy you have borrowed (see suggestions on page **74**), one for each student

- Copies of the following, one for each student:
  - "What to Do If It Happens to You" (page **118**)
  - "Sample Informal Resolution Letter" (page **119**)
  - "Sexual Harassment Survey" (pages **134–138**)
  - "Course Evaluation" (pages **139–140**)

- Copies of the following, one of each:
  - Case Studies: Secondary Schools (pages **120–126**)
  - Case Studies: Workplaces (pages **127–132**).

SUPPLEMENTAL ACTIVITIES

Unit Three supplemental activities are found on pages **112–114**.

1. STUDENT ACTIVITY: ASSUMPTIONS AND ATTITUDES

▸ Distribute the "Assumptions and Attitudes" note cards to randomly selected students.

▸ If necessary, explain the meaning of "assumption" (something that is taken for granted; something that is accepted as true, even if no real proof exists to support this belief).

▸ Have each student read his/her card aloud and tell how that particular assumption or attitude could affect a victim of sexual harassment.

2. STUDENT ACTIVITY: EFFECTS ON THE VICTIM

▸ Divide the class into four groups, A, B, C, and D. Give flip chart paper and markers to each group.

▸ Instruct the students in Group A to brainstorm and list ways in which sexual harassment could affect a victim *physically*. Explain that being sexually harassed is very stressful and can lead to a variety of stress-related physical symptoms and problems.

▸ Instruct the students in Group B to brainstorm and list ways in which sexual harassment could affect a victim *emotionally*. (Boys may have more difficulty with this than girls, so you may want to suggest that they imagine how they would feel if their girlfriend was harassed, or remember how they felt when someone treated them disrespectfully.)

▸ Instruct the students in Group C to brainstorm and list ways in which sexual harassment could affect a victim's *school performance* and *school experience*.

▸ Instruct the students in Group D to brainstorm and list ways in which sexual harassment could affect a victim's *future*.

▸ Tell the students to keep in mind that the effects of harassment may vary, depending on whether the harasser is a peer (another student) or someone in a position of authority (a teacher, staff person, employer, etc.).

▸ Allow a few moments for the students to compile their lists.

▸ Post the lists on the wall for all to see. Bring the groups back together again. Have a spokesperson from each group read their list aloud.

▸ If the students did not include the examples on page 14 on their lists, bring them to their attention. You might say, "What about _____," or "Do you think that _____ might be another (physical, emotional, school, future) effect of sexual harassment?" Save discussion of self-blaming for the next section.

- Show Transparency #20, "Effects of Sexual Harassment" (page 115). Read it aloud to the students.

- Suggested script:

  > (1) *Sexual harassment can have very serious effects on its victims. It isn't something that most people can just ignore. Even if they could ignore it, that wouldn't make the harassment stop. Sexual harassment gets worse when it is ignored.*

  > (2) *Sexual harassment isn't sexual assault, unless it involves unwanted touching. But most victims of sexual harassment report having the same feelings as victims of sexual assault. Remember that sexual harassment and sexual assault, including rape, are on the same continuum of sexual violence.*

3. VICTIMS BLAME THEMSELVES

  > (1) *Victims of sexual harassment and sexual assault tend to blame themselves. They actually believe that the assault or harassment happened because of the way they were dressed, or because of something they said or did.*

  > (2) *Or they believe it happened because of something they didn't do or say. Either way, they see it as their fault.*

  > (3) *What are some other reasons why victims blame themselves?*

- Allow a few moments for ideas and discussion.

- Suggested script:

  > (4) *In fact, sexual harassment is never, ever the victim's fault. Neither is sexual assault. No crime is ever the victim's fault. It is the fault of the person who did it.*

II. HOW SEXUAL HARASSMENT AFFECTS THE ORGANIZATION

1. EFFECTS ON THE LEARNING/WORK ENVIRONMENT

- Suggested script:

  > *Sexual harassment doesn't just hurt the victims. It hurts the places where it happens—including schools and organizations. Who can give examples?*

- Allow a few moments for examples. If the students don't mention those given on page 11, bring them to their attention.

2. THE COSTS OF SEXUAL HARASSMENT

▶ Show Transparency #21, "The Costs of Sexual Harassment" (page 116). Read it aloud to the students.

▶ Suggested script:

> (1) *Sexual harassment costs American businesses millions of dollars each year. The figures shown here don't even include the costs of going to court, hiring lawyers, and paying the victim if the company loses the case.*

> (2) *The average costs of an EEOC sexual harassment case that goes to trial is $80,000, with anywhere from $4,000 to $25,000 extra in witness fees, depositions, and other costs.*

> (3) *Schools are starting to pay the costs of sexual harassment. In 1991, a high school in Minnesota was ordered to pay $15,000 to a student who was sexually harassed by her male peers.*

> (4) *Sexual harassment can also cost victims a lot of money. They may have to pay for lawyers to represent them in court and take time off from work. The high cost of taking legal action is one reason why many victims don't report the harassment. We'll explore some other reasons later on.*

III. EXAMINING YOUR SCHOOL OR DISTRICT'S SEXUAL HARASSMENT POLICY

1. IF YOUR SCHOOL OR DISTRICT HAS A SEXUAL HARASSMENT POLICY...

▶ Distribute copies to the students.

2. IF YOUR SCHOOL OR DISTRICT DOES NOT HAVE A SEXUAL HARASSMENT POLICY...

▶ Distribute copies of the sample policy you have acquired from another source.

3. EXAMINING THE POLICY

▶ Examine the policy with the students. Instruct the students to read the entire policy or suggested portions, depending on length.

▶ Invite students to comment on anything that seems unclear, confusing, or misleading. Record their comments. Tell the students that you will present their comments to your school or district (or to the place the policy was borrowed from) at the end of this program. Be sure to follow through!

1. EXAMINING AN EXISTING PROCEDURE

▸ Suggested script:

> (1) *Now that we've read through the policy, let's go back and pay special attention to the procedure for reporting incidents of sexual harassment.*

> (2) *Is the procedure clear? Does it make it relatively easy for a victim to report a sexual harassment incident? Explain your answer.*

▸ Allow a few moments for responses.

▸ Suggested script:

> (3) *Who are victims supposed to report to? This person is usually called the "complaint manager," Title IX coordinator, or Human Rights officer. Do you agree that this person makes a good complaint manager? Why or why not?*

▸ Allow a few moments for responses.

▸ Suggested script:

> (4) *If you were in charge of writing our school's sexual harassment policy, what staff people would you name as complaint managers? Think of people you trust and respect.*

▸ Allow a few moments for suggestions. Afterward, tell the students that these trusted, respected individuals might also be good people to go to and tell about incidents of sexual harassment, even if they aren't official complaint managers.

2. WHAT TO DO IF IT HAPPENS TO YOU

▸ Hand out copies of "What to Do If It Happens to You" (page **118**), one to each student.

▸ Read it aloud to the students, or ask for volunteers.

▸ Suggested script:

> (1) *How does this procedure compare to the one we just reviewed? How is it the same? How is it different?* (Many existing procedures are inadequate. They do not provide enough information, or enough specific information, about what victims should do when they are harassed, or how they should report the harassment.)

(2) *This procedure explains how to document harassment—how to keep a careful written record of it. This is very important! If you are ever a victim of harassment, people will take your claim more seriously if you can say, "This is what happened, on these dates and at these times...." They will take you less seriously if you can't provide the details.*

(3) *Documentation is especially important for victims who decide to take legal action against their harassers. It serves as a proof of sorts that the harassment really happened.*

(4) *Documentation is also important for victims who want to take any other kind of action against their harassers, including formal and informal complaints that are handled internally—in the school or workplace. It helps to support the victims' claims that harassment has occurred.*

3. INFORMAL RESOLUTION

▶ Suggested script:

(1) *Most victims of sexual harassment just want the harassment to stop. They may not want to file a formal complaint or take legal action.*

(2) *Sometimes it's enough to talk to the harasser. Tell the person how his or her behavior is affecting you. Tell the person that you want the behavior to stop—right now. Bring someone along to support you, if that makes you feel safer and more comfortable.*

(3) *For some people, talking to the harasser is not an option. This is too hard for them to do. They feel powerless and afraid. They don't want to confront the person who is the cause of these feelings.*

(4) *There is another option available: writing a letter to the harasser.*

▶ Hand out copies of the "Sample Informal Resolution Letter" (page **119**), one for each student.

▶ Suggested script:

(5) *This is a letter that could have been written by a victim to her harasser. Notice that it includes four specific things: first, a description of the harassing behavior; second, how it makes the victim feel; third, the consequences the victim has experienced as a result of the behavior; and fourth, a request that the harasser stop the behavior.*

(6) *The victim makes two copies of the letter and keeps one for herself. She gives the other copy to the harasser in private, with only one other person present: a trusted adult. This can be a teacher, a supervisor, or someone else the victim asks to be there. The adult doesn't have to do anything—just be there. This shows support for the victim and emphasizes that this is a serious matter.*

(7) *Talking to the harasser, or writing a letter, is called* informal resolution. *Either one is a positive, effective action to take. It gives you a way to deal with the problem on your own terms, in your own words. It gives the harasser a chance to stop the behavior before it goes any further. It gives everyone an alternative to legal action.*

(8) *Informal resolution empowers the victim. It encourages the harasser to take responsibility for the behavior and apologize for it. And it takes place in a safe, confidential setting.*

(9) *Informal resolution doesn't always work. But it's almost always a good place to start.*

4. WHY VICTIMS DON'T REPORT SEXUAL HARASSMENT

▸ Suggested script:

(1) *If somebody stole your car or robbed your house, you would report the crime. Auto theft and burglary are both against the law.*

(2) *Sexual harassment is illegal, yet many victims never report it.*

▸ Show Transparency #22, "Why Victims Don't Report Sexual Harassment" (page 117). Read it aloud to the students.

▸ Suggested script:

(3) *What are some ways you could support a friend who had been sexually harassed? What could you say? What could you do?*

▸ Allow a few moments for responses and discussion. If students don't mention, "Encourage her/him to report the harassment," bring it to their attention.

5. CONSIDERING THE CONSEQUENCES

▸ Suggested script:

(1) *Sometimes victims don't report sexual harassment because they think it doesn't matter. Nothing ever happens to harassers. Why bother reporting?*

(2) *This is another reason why every school/district and organization should have a sexual harassment policy. This policy should spell out the consequences for harassing behaviors.*

(3) *Consequences can help harassers choose to stop harassing. If they know they can get into trouble—and exactly what kind of trouble—they may decide that it isn't worth it to keep harassing.*

(4) *What would be some appropriate consequences for sexual harassment? Give examples.*

- Allow a few moments for responses. Suggest the following if the students don't mention them, and invite comments:

  - The harasser must apologize to the victim

  - If the harasser is a student: School suspension

  - If the harasser is an athlete: Being barred from games and competitions for a period of time (or the rest of the school year)

  - If the harasser is an adult: The victim takes legal action against him or her

  - If the harasser is an adult: Loss of job; loss of reputation; going to jail; paying a fine.

V. SEXUAL HARASSMENT CASE STUDIES

1. SEXUAL HARASSMENT IN SECONDARY SCHOOLS

- Divide the class into small groups. Hand out the seven Secondary School Case Studies (pages **120–126**). Distribute all of the case studies; some groups may have more than one.

- Suggested script:

  (1) *Let's take what we've learned about sexual harassment, policy, and procedure and apply it to real life.*

  (2) *These case studies describe incidents that actually took place in high schools in the United States. Read your case study and answer the questions.*

- Allow about 10 minutes for this activity.

- Ask someone from each group to read their case study/studies aloud to the class and give their answers. Discuss how they arrived at their answers. (For example, why should the victim tell a teacher?) Compare their answers to the answer key on pages **107–109**. Allow a few moments for comments and discussion.

- If there is time, ask students to reply to these additional questions for one or more cases:

  - Could this situation have been prevented? Explain. (Tell students to avoid blaming the victim.)

  - How would you feel if you were the victim in this situation?

  - What would you do if you were the victim?

  - What would be your greatest concern/fear?

  - What if the victim was your friend, and you disagreed with what he/she decided to do following the incident?

  - Why is it important for people to support one another in cases like this?

2. SEXUAL HARASSMENT IN WORKPLACES

▶ Hand out the six Workplace Case Studies (pages **127–132**). Distribute all of the case studies; some groups may have more than one.

▶ Suggested script:

> *These case studies describe incidents that have occurred to people in different jobs in different companies. Read your case study and answer the questions.*

▶ Allow about 10 minutes for this activity.

▶ Ask someone from each group to read their case study/studies aloud to the class and give their answers. Discuss how they arrived at their answers. (For example, why should the victim tell the manager or supervisor?) Compare their answers to the answer key on pages **109–111**. Allow a few moments for comments and discussion.

▶ If there is time, ask students to reply to these additional questions for one or more cases:

- Could this situation have been prevented? Explain. (Tell students to avoid blaming the victim.)

- How would you feel if you were the victim in this situation?

- What would you do if you were the victim?

- What would be your greatest concern/fear?

- What if the victim was your friend or coworker, and you disagreed with what he/she decided to do following the incident?

- Why is it important for people to support one another in cases like this?

VI. RIGHTS AND RESPONSIBILITIES

▶ Divide the class into four groups, A, B, C, and D. Give flip chart paper and markers to each group.

▶ Instruct the students in Group A to brainstorm a list of ideas on the topic, "Sexual Harassment and Student Rights." (Examples: Every student has the right to a safe learning environment. Every student has the right to be treated with respect.)

▶ Instruct the students in Group B to brainstorm a list of ideas on the topic, "Sexual Harassment and Student Responsibilities." (Examples: Every student is responsible for abiding by school rules concerning sexual harassment. Every student is responsible for treating others with respect.)

- Instruct the students in Group C to brainstorm a list of ideas on the topic, "Sexual Harassment and the Rights of Schools" (or Workplaces). (Example: Every school has the right to establish a code of conduct for students and staff.)

- Instruct the students in Group D to brainstorm a list of ideas on the topic, "Sexual Harassment and School Responsibilities" (or Workplace Responsibilities). (Example: Every school is responsible for providing a safe learning environment.)

- Tell each group to write their ideas on flip chart paper. Allow no more than 10 minutes for this activity.

- Post the lists on the wall. Bring the groups back together again. Have a spokesperson from each group read their list aloud.

- Allow a few moments for responses, questions, and discussion.

- Suggested script:

  (1) *You have the right to be in a safe environment, at school and in the workplace. You have the right to be treated with dignity and respect.*

  (2) *You also have the responsibility to treat others with dignity and respect.*

VII. ENDING THE UNIT

1. SEXUAL HARASSMENT SURVEY

- Distribute copies of the "Sexual Harassment Survey" (pages **134–138**), one to each student.

- Suggested script:

  (1) *We have spent the past few days talking about sexual harassment in schools and workplaces. Do you think it is a problem in our school? Here is your chance to do something about it. You can participate in a survey about sexual harassment in our school.*

  (2) *You don't have to sign your name. The information you provide will be kept confidential. Nobody will know that the information came from you—you will remain anonymous. But the more information you provide, and the more accurate it is, the more you will help our school to prevent and stop sexual harassment from happening here.*

  (3) *Please complete your survey and return it within the next few days.*

- Tell the students where to bring their completed surveys. Suggestions: a drop box in your office; your mail slot in the school office; by mail to your attention at your school address.

2. PROGRAM SUMMARY

▸ Summarize *Sexual Harassment and Teens* by reviewing the unit objectives (pages **40**, **64**, and **96**).

▸ Allow a few moments for questions, comments, and discussion.

▸ Distribute copies of the "Course Evaluation" (pages **139–140**), one to each student.

▸ Suggested script:

(1) *Please complete this evaluation form and return it as soon as possible. It's like the survey in that you don't have to sign your name, but it's different because it's a lot shorter!*

(2) *We really want to know what you thought of this course. Your responses are very important! They will help us to do a better job next time.*

▸ Conclude by thanking the students for participating in the program.

CASE STUDY: SECONDARY SCHOOL #1

John and his classmates were happy....

1. Is this sexual harassment? *Yes*

2. What behaviors tell you that it is or isn't? *Unwanted touch, exposure of John's genitals to class*

3. Who is the harasser? *John's "friends"*

4. Who is the victim? *John*

5. What can or should the victim do about this incident? Check any that apply:
   Tell a friend, teacher, school counselor, principal, parent/guardian; write an informal resolution letter to the harasser; follow school policy; get someone else to talk to the harasser (a school staff member)

CASE STUDY: SECONDARY SCHOOL #2

A junior high gym teacher became very angry....

1. Is this sexual harassment? *Yes*

2. What behaviors tell you that it is or isn't? *When girls do jumping-jacks, their breasts move; because they are made to do it in front of the boys, this is exploitative behavior; it is an abuse of power by the gym teacher; it is also sex discrimination, because boys are made to do push-ups, which are physically harder than jumping-jacks.*

3. Who is the harasser? *The gym teacher*

4. Who is the victim? *The girls and boys*

5. What can or should the victim do about this incident? Check any that apply:
   Tell a friend, school counselor, principal, their parents/guardians; get someone else to talk to the harasser (the principal, parents)

CASE STUDY: SECONDARY SCHOOL #3

The whole school was excited: Their wrestling team....

1. Is this sexual harassment? *Yes*

2. What behaviors tell you that it is or isn't? *Cornering the cheerleader in the bathroom; making comments about her body*

3. Who is the harasser? *The wrestlers*

4. Who is the victim? *The cheerleader*

5. What can or should the victim do about this incident? Check any that apply: *Tell a friend, school counselor, principal, her parents/guardians; write an informal resolution letter to the harassers; follow school policy*

NOTE: Although this incident occurred outside the school, the school is still legally responsible because it happened during a school-sponsored event.

CASE STUDY: SECONDARY SCHOOL #4

During a powder-puff football game....

1. Is this sexual harassment? *Yes*

2. What behaviors tell you that it is or isn't? *Sexual cheers; the power of the crowd*

3. Who is the harasser? *The cheerleaders and the audience members who joined in the cheering*

4. Who is the victim? *The players and the audience members who found the cheering offensive*

5. What can or should the victim do about this incident? Check any that apply: *Tell the principal; write an informal resolution letter to the harassers; follow school policy; tell school board members*

CASE STUDY: SECONDARY SCHOOL #5

During lunch break, female students walk down the hallway....

1. Is this sexual harassment? *Yes*

2. What behaviors tell you that it is or isn't? *Comments; rating scale*

3. Who is the harasser? *The boys in the hall*

4. Who is the victim? *The girls*

5. What can or should the victim do about this incident? Check any that apply: *Tell the school counselor, principal; follow school policy; get someone else to talk to the harassers (a school staff member)*

CASE STUDY: SECONDARY SCHOOL #6

As an extra-credit project for a drama class....

1. Is this sexual harassment? *Yes*

2. What behaviors tell you that it is or isn't? *Sexually explicit movie*

3. Who is the harasser? *The students who brought in the movie; the teacher who allowed it to be shown in class*

4. Who is the victim? *The girl who felt uncomfortable and complained*

5. What can or should the victim do about this incident? Check any that apply: *Tell the teacher, school counselor, principal, parent/guardian; follow school policy; get someone else to talk to the harassers (a school staff member)*

CASE STUDY: SECONDARY SCHOOL #7

Between classes and during lunch break, it isn't uncommon to see couples....

1. Is this sexual harassment? *Yes*

2. What behaviors tell you that it is or isn't? *Making out in public places so others can see*

3. Who is the harasser? *The couples*

4. Who is the victim? *Other students and staff*

5. What can or should the victim do about this incident? Check any that apply: *Tell a friend, school counselor, principal, parent/guardian; follow school policy; get someone else to talk to the harassers (a school staff member)*

CASE STUDIES: WORKPLACES ANSWER KEY

CASE STUDY: WORKPLACE #1

Bob, the groundskeeper at the local country club....

1. Is this sexual harassment? *No*

2. What behaviors tell you that it is or isn't? *They have been dating for a year. They agreed to move in together. Their difference in power at work (Tricia is the golf pro; Bob the groundskeeper) doesn't matter to them.*

CASE STUDY: WORKPLACE #2

Julie is the only woman account executive...

1. Is this sexual harassment? *Yes—with a broader definition that also includes sex discrimination*

2. What behaviors tell you that it is or isn't? *Julie is the only female at the meetings; she is always given the duty typically thought of as secretarial/women's work*

3. Who is the harasser? *Jack*

4. Who is the victim? *Julie*

5. Who is legally responsible for the harassment? *Jack and the business*

6. What can or should the victim do? Check any that apply: *Tell the manager/supervisor (Jack); if that doesn't work, go to his boss*

CASE STUDY: WORKPLACE #3

Ms. Tory Olson has been promised a promotion...

1. Is this sexual harassment? *Yes*

2. What behaviors tell you that it is or isn't? *Implying that decisions about Ms. Olson's employment will be based on whether or not she goes along; boss has power over Ms. Olson*

3. Who is the harasser? *Ms. Olson's boss*

4. Who is the victim? *Ms. Olson*

5. Who is legally responsible for the harassment? *Ms. Olson's boss and the business*

6. What can or should the victim do? Check any that apply: *Tell a friend; follow workplace policy; file an official complaint*

CASE STUDY: WORKPLACE #4

Susan is a sales clerk at the auto shop....

1. Is this sexual harassment? *Yes*

2. What behaviors tell you that it is or isn't? *Sexual comments and pictures on the walls*

3. Who is the harasser? *The men Susan works with*

4. Who is the victim? *Susan*

5. Who is legally responsible for the harassment? *The other mechanics, the boss, and the business*

6. What can or should the victim do? Check any that apply: *Tell a friend; follow workplace policy; file an official complaint*

CASE STUDY: WORKPLACE #5

Mark has been trying to break off his relationship with his boss, Ed....

1. Is this sexual harassment? *Yes*

2. What behaviors tell you that it is or isn't? *A sexual relationship carried into the workplace; Ed (boss) has power over Mark*

3. Who is the harasser? *Ed*

4. Who is the victim? *Mark*

5. Who is legally responsible for the harassment? *Ed and the business*

6. What can or should the victim do? Check any that apply: *Tell a friend; follow workplace policy; tell a representative from Human Resources; file an official complaint*

CASE STUDY: WORKPLACE #6

Dr. Fran Kelhoffer, Chief of Staff at the local hospital....

1. Is this sexual harassment? *Yes*

2. What behaviors tell you that it is or isn't? *Dr. Kelhoffer's power position over the new doctor*

3. Who is the harasser? *Dr. Kelhoffer*

4. Who is the victim? *The new doctor*

5. Who is legally responsible for the harassment? *Dr. Kelhoffer and the hospital*

6. What can or should the victim do? Check any that apply: *Follow workplace policy; write an informal resolution letter to Dr. Kelhoffer; tell a representative from Human Resources*

NOTE: Asking a coworker for a date, even after hours and at a social function, may influence the working relationship. This case might be considered differently if Dr. Kelhoffer were not in a position of power over the new doctor.

QUESTIONS FOR DISCUSSION

1. What are the two most important things to remember if you are sexually harassed? *(It isn't your fault, and don't ignore the harassment.)*

2. Do you think that girls/women usually ignore sexual harassment? Explain.

3. Do you think that boys/men usually ignore sexual harassment? Explain.

4. Is there pressure for girls/women to put up with sexual harassment? Is there pressure for girls/women to harass boys/men? How do these pressures compare?

5. How can you tell a harasser to stop harassing you?

6. If telling the harasser to stop doesn't work, what should you do next?

7. Should you pretend to go along with unwanted sexual attention? Should you laugh and joke about it? Why or why not?

8. What could a boy/man do to prevent his friends from sexually harassing someone?

9. Do you think that schools have a responsibility for doing something about sexual harassment? Explain. Do you think teachers have a responsibility? Explain.

10. Do you think that students have a responsibility for doing something about sexual harassment? Explain.

SETTING POLICY

If your school or district does not have a sexual harassment policy, invite students to develop one. They should be sure to include the names of key staff members they feel they could trust to act as complaint managers.

Help the students present their policy to your school or district. Work with them to implement the policy.

REMEMBER WHEN

Tell the students to think back to a time when they were sexually harassed (or their girlfriend/boyfriend was sexually harassed). Have them write a letter to the harasser describing:

- what the harasser did that was offensive

- when it happened

- how it made the victim feel

- any consequences the victim experienced.

Tell the students that they may destroy the letter after they finish writing it, if they wish. Those who are willing may share their letters with the class, omitting the name of the harasser (and the victim, if they wrote about someone else's experience).

PLAYWRITING

Have the students write a play or script about sexual harassment, sex role stereotypes, or another related topic and perform it before an audience.

SEXUAL HARASSMENT IN THE NEWS

Have the students collect newspaper and magazine articles about sexual harassment and bring them to school. Display them on the school or class bulletin board.

ARTICLE WRITING

Encourage students to write articles for the school newspaper about sexual harassment in the schools. Or they might write about this program—what they learned, what they experienced, how it changed their perceptions about sexual harassment, how it affected their behavior.

PREVENTION WEEK

Work through the student council to sponsor a Sexual Harassment Prevention Week. Ideas: Present *Sexual Harassment and Teens* as an evening program so parents and community members can attend. Hold a poster contest. Hold a writing contest. Present plays, skits, and role plays. Produce a video or a public service announcement. Ask local leaders to pass a Stop Sexual Harassment proclamation.

YOUNG AMBASSADORS

Consider your class of program "graduates." Are there any athletes, student council members, organization presidents, or other leaders—or students with leadership abilities? Any students who enjoy special status among their peers and within the community? Were these students responsive to *Sexual Harassment and Teens*? Did this program appear to change their perceptions and affect their behavior?

If so, consider asking them to speak on sexual harassment to junior high/middle school students. A sensitive and aware older student can make a wonderful ambassador to younger kids.

SUPPORT GROUP

Start a support group for students who are enrolled in nontraditional classes; students who have had personal experience with sexual harassment; and/or students who are frustrated with sexism in the schools.

STUDENT HANDBOOK EVALUATION

Evaluate the student handbook according to Title IX criteria.

NO LAUGHING MATTER

Distribute copies of "No Laughing Matter: High School Students & Sexual Harassment" (page **133**). Read it and discuss it with the students.

EFFECTS OF SEXUAL HARASSMENT

- **83 percent of women in the workplace said that sexual harassment had interfered with their ability to do their work**

- **65 percent experienced physical stress symptoms**

(Working Woman Institute)

THE COSTS OF SEXUAL HARASSMENT

- The average major American business spends $6.7 million a year on indirect sexual harassment costs including:

  - loss of productivity

  - increased absenteeism

  - increased employee turnover

- The federal government spent $267 million in two years on the same indirect costs

- K-Mart paid out $3.2 million in 1987.

None of these costs include litigation.

(*Working Woman* magazine)

WHY VICTIMS DON'T REPORT SEXUAL HARASSMENT

- They blame themselves

- They feel helpless, hopeless, and/or powerless

- They don't know how to report the harassment

- They think that their complaint won't be taken seriously

- They don't trust their own perceptions of what happened—maybe they "misunderstood"

- They don't want to "rock the boat"

- They are afraid of the harasser or others (example: the harasser's friends or family)

- They don't trust "the system"

- They don't think their school/workplace will support them if they report the harassment

- They don't think their friends will support them

- They feel embarrassed

- They don't think that reporting will make any difference; they don't believe that anything will be done about the harassment or the harasser

- They don't want to get the harasser into trouble

- They are prevented or blocked by sex role stereotyping

- They are prevented or blocked by victim behavior

WHAT TO DO
IF IT HAPPENS TO YOU

Follow the sexual harassment policy and procedure that is used by your school, district, or workplace. If there is no existing policy and procedure, use this one.

Step 1: Communicate to your harasser 1) what you are feeling, and 2) that you expect the behavior to stop. You may do this verbally or in writing. (See the "Sample Informal Resolution Letter" handout.) If you choose, you may get help and support from a friend, parent, professional, or other trusted adult.

Step 2: If the behavior is repeated, go to a person in authority, such as a principal, counselor, complaint manager, or supervisor. Document exactly what happened. Give a copy of your written record to the authority, and keep one for yourself.

Your documentation should include the following information. Use exact quotes where appropriate and whenever possible.

- what happened
- when it happened
- where it happened
- who did the harassing
- who the witnesses were (if any)
- what you said and/or did in response to the harassment
- how your harasser responded to you
- how you felt about the harassment

Step 3: If the behavior is repeated again, go to a person in higher authority, such as a school board member, the superintendent of schools, the company president, etc. Keep documenting the behavior.

At any point in this process, you may choose to contact the Office of Civil Rights, your State Department of Education, your State Department of Human Rights, an attorney, or a police officer.

RESOURCE AGENCIES

1. Office of Civil Rights _____
   Telephone number

2. Department of Education _____
   Telephone number

3. Department of Human Rights _____
   Telephone number

4. Local Program for Victims of Sexual Assault _____
   Telephone number

5. Police/Sheriff's Department _____
   Telephone number

Sexual Harassment and Teens, copyright © 1992 Susan Strauss. Free Spirit Publishing Inc. This page may be reproduced.

SAMPLE INFORMAL RESOLUTION LETTER

September 26, 1992

John Doe:

When I walk to math class on Mondays, I pass your locker. You wink at me and make rude noises and ask me if I want to have sex with you.

Your behavior makes me feel angry and humiliated. I feel embarrassed in front of my friends.

Because I have to pass your locker, I feel anxious about walking to math class. It's hard for me to concentrate on my school work.

I want you to stop this behavior, starting now. Don't wink at me anymore or make those noises or ask me if I want to have sex with you.

Sincerely,

Jane Doe

CASE STUDY: SECONDARY SCHOOL #1

John and his classmates were happy to go on a special swimming trip sponsored by their school. Their school was quite old and did not have a swimming pool.

After swimming for a short time, John decided to get out to buy a soda. As he walked around the outside of the pool, two of his male friends ran up on either side of him, grabbed the waist of his swim trunks, and pulled them down to his knees.

Questions

1. Is this sexual harassment?   YES   NO

2. What behaviors tell you that it is or isn't? _____

_____

3. Who is the harasser? _____

4. Who is the victim? _____

5. What can or should the victim do about this incident? Check any that apply:

__ Tell a friend

__ Tell a teacher (or other trusted school staff member)

__ Tell the school counselor

__ Tell the principal

__ Tell a parent/guardian

__ Ignore it

__ Take legal action (such as calling the police or a lawyer)

__ Write an informal resolution letter to the harasser

__ Drop the class

__ Join a support group

__ Follow the school sexual harassment policy and procedure

__ Get someone else to talk to the harasser

__ Other (describe): _____

_____

_____

CASE STUDY: SECONDARY SCHOOL #2

A junior high gym teacher became very angry if his students were tardy for class. He made them do extra exercises as punishment for their tardiness. The boys had to do push-ups while the girls watched; the girls had to do jumping-jacks in front of the boys.

Questions

1. Is this sexual harassment?   YES   NO

2. What behaviors tell you that it is or isn't? _____

_____

3. Who is the harasser? _____

4. Who is the victim? _____

5. What can or should the victim do about this incident? Check any that apply:

__ Tell a friend

__ Tell a teacher (or other trusted school staff member)

__ Tell the school counselor

__ Tell the principal

__ Tell a parent/guardian

__ Ignore it

__ Take legal action (such as calling the police or a lawyer)

__ Write an informal resolution letter to the harasser

__ Drop the class

__ Join a support group

__ Follow the school sexual harassment policy and procedure

__ Get someone else to talk to the harasser

__ Other (describe): _____

_____

_____

CASE STUDY: SECONDARY SCHOOL #3

The whole school was excited: Their wrestling team was going to the state tournament! Three of the wrestlers were competing in three different weight groups.

All three won their first competition. They showered and returned to the auditorium to watch the rest of the tournament. During a break, they followed one of their school cheerleaders out into the hallway, pushed her into the bathroom, and made sexual comments about how great she looked in her cheerleading uniform.

Questions

1. Is this sexual harassment?   YES   NO

2. What behaviors tell you that it is or isn't? _____

_____

3. Who is the harasser? _____

4. Who is the victim? _____

5. What can or should the victim do about this incident? Check any that apply:

___ Tell a friend

___ Tell a teacher (or other trusted school staff member)

___ Tell the school counselor

___ Tell the principal

___ Tell a parent/guardian

___ Ignore it

___ Take legal action (such as calling the police or a lawyer)

___ Write an informal resolution letter to the harasser

___ Drop the class

___ Join a support group

___ Follow the school sexual harassment policy and procedure

___ Get someone else to talk to the harasser

___ Other (describe): _____

_____

_____

CASE STUDY: SECONDARY SCHOOL #4

During a powder-puff football game (in which the girls play football and the boys cheer), the male cheerleaders yelled cheers about the girl's "tits" and "asses" to an audience of students, parents, and school staff.

Questions

1. Is this sexual harassment?   YES   NO

2. What behaviors tell you that it is or isn't? _____

_____

3. Who is the harasser? _____

4. Who is the victim? _____

5. What can or should the victim do about this incident? Check any that apply:

__ Tell a friend

__ Tell a teacher (or other trusted school staff member)

__ Tell the school counselor

__ Tell the principal

__ Tell a parent/guardian

__ Ignore it

__ Take legal action (such as calling the police or a lawyer)

__ Write an informal resolution letter to the harasser

__ Drop the class

__ Join a support group

__ Follow the school sexual harassment policy and procedure

__ Get someone else to talk to the harasser

__ Other (describe): _____

_____

_____

CASE STUDY:
SECONDARY SCHOOL #5

During lunch break, female students walk down the hallway to the school's break area. Male students frequently congregate along the hallway and make comments about the girls' appearance as they pass. They rate the girls on a scale of 1–10.

Questions

1. Is this sexual harassment?   YES   NO

2. What behaviors tell you that it is or isn't? _____

_____

3. Who is the harasser? _____

4. Who is the victim? _____

5. What can or should the victim do about this incident? Check any that apply:

___ Tell a friend

___ Tell a teacher (or other trusted school staff member)

___ Tell the school counselor

___ Tell the principal

___ Tell a parent/guardian

___ Ignore it

___ Take legal action (such as calling the police or a lawyer)

___ Write an informal resolution letter to the harasser

___ Drop the class

___ Join a support group

___ Follow the school sexual harassment policy and procedure

___ Get someone else to talk to the harasser

___ Other (describe): _____

_____

_____

CASE STUDY:
SECONDARY SCHOOL #6

As an extra-credit project for a drama class, two students brought in an R-rated video for the class to watch. The video contained sexually violent and explicit scenes. It took three class periods to watch the whole movie. One of the students felt very uncomfortable during the movie and complained.

Questions

1. Is this sexual harassment?   YES   NO

2. What behaviors tell you that it is or isn't? _____

_____

3. Who is the harasser? _____

4. Who is the victim? _____

5. What can or should the victim do about this incident? Check any that apply:

__ Tell a friend

__ Tell a teacher (or other trusted school staff member)

__ Tell the school counselor

__ Tell the principal

__ Tell a parent/guardian

__ Ignore it

__ Take legal action (such as calling the police or a lawyer)

__ Write an informal resolution letter to the harasser

__ Drop the class

__ Join a support group

__ Follow the school sexual harassment policy and procedure

__ Get someone else to talk to the harasser

__ Other (describe): _____

_____

_____

CASE STUDY: SECONDARY SCHOOL #7

Between classes and during lunch break, it isn't uncommon to see couples making out (kissing, hugging, touching) in the school hallways. Some students ignore it; some students laugh about it; some students feel embarrassed about it.

Questions

1. Is this sexual harassment?   YES   NO

2. What behaviors tell you that it is or isn't? _____

_____

3. Who is the harasser? _____

4. Who is the victim? _____

5. What can or should the victim do about this incident? Check any that apply:

__ Tell a friend

__ Tell a teacher (or other trusted school staff member)

__ Tell the school counselor

__ Tell the principal

__ Tell a parent/guardian

__ Ignore it

__ Take legal action (such as calling the police or a lawyer)

__ Write an informal resolution letter to the harasser

__ Drop the class

__ Join a support group

__ Follow the school sexual harassment policy and procedure

__ Get someone else to talk to the harasser

__ Other (describe): _____

_____

_____

CASE STUDY: WORKPLACE #1

Bob, the groundskeeper at the local country club, has been dating Tricia, the golf pro, for the last year. They have recently decided to move in together.

Questions

1. Is this sexual harassment?   YES   NO

2. What behaviors tell you that it is or isn't? _____

_____

3. Who is the harasser? _____

4. Who is the victim? _____

5. Who is legally responsible for the harassment? _____

6. What can or should the victim do? Check any that apply:

__ Tell a friend

__ Tell the manager/supervisor

__ Tell a representative from the Human Resources Department

__ Ignore it

__ Follow the workplace sexual harassment policy and procedure

__ File an official complaint (take legal action)

__ Write an informal resolution letter to the harasser

__ Quit the job

__ Get someone else to talk to the harasser

__ Other (describe): _____

_____

_____

CASE STUDY: WORKPLACE #2

Julie is the only woman account executive who is involved in the monthly management meetings. Jack, the chairman, always asks her to take the minutes of the meetings.

Questions

1. Is this sexual harassment?　　YES　　NO

2. What behaviors tell you that it is or isn't? _____

_____

3. Who is the harasser? _____

4. Who is the victim? _____

5. Who is legally responsible for the harassment? _____

6. What can or should the victim do? Check any that apply:

___ Tell a friend

___ Tell the manager/supervisor

___ Tell a representative from the Human Resources Department

___ Ignore it

___ Follow the workplace sexual harassment policy and procedure

___ File an official complaint (take legal action)

___ Write an informal resolution letter to the harasser

___ Quit the job

___ Get someone else to talk to the harasser

___ Other (describe): _____

_____

_____

CASE STUDY: WORKPLACE #3

Ms. Tory Olson has been promised a promotion and a raise by her boss. He has implied that she will receive them only if she agrees to have a few after-hours dinners with him.

Questions

1. Is this sexual harassment?   YES   NO

2. What behaviors tell you that it is or isn't? _____

_____

3. Who is the harasser? _____

4. Who is the victim? _____

5. Who is legally responsible for the harassment? _____

6. What can or should the victim do? Check any that apply:

__ Tell a friend

__ Tell the manager/supervisor

__ Tell a representative from the Human Resources Department

__ Ignore it

__ Follow the workplace sexual harassment policy and procedure

__ File an official complaint (take legal action)

__ Write an informal resolution letter to the harasser

__ Quit the job

__ Get someone else to talk to the harasser

__ Other (describe): _____

_____

_____

CASE STUDY: WORKPLACE #4

Susan is a sales clerk at the auto shop. Many of the mechanics make sexual comments to her during the day. Plus there are pictures of nude women on the walls. Susan has complained to her boss, but he tells her that she has to expect that kind of behavior when she works with all men.

Questions

1. Is this sexual harassment?   YES   NO

2. What behaviors tell you that it is or isn't? _____

_____

3. Who is the harasser? _____

4. Who is the victim? _____

5. Who is legally responsible for the harassment? _____

6. What can or should the victim do? Check any that apply:

__ Tell a friend

__ Tell the manager/supervisor

__ Tell a representative from the Human Resources Department

__ Ignore it

__ Follow the workplace sexual harassment policy and procedure

__ File an official complaint (take legal action)

__ Write an informal resolution letter to the harasser

__ Quit the job

__ Get someone else to talk to the harasser

__ Other (describe): _____

_____

_____

CASE STUDY: WORKPLACE #5

Mark has been trying to break off his relationship with his boss, Ed. Ed is having a tough time accepting Mark's decision to end their affair. Ed has told Mark that if he continues to be so hard to get along with, Ed will fire him.

Questions

1. Is this sexual harassment?   YES   NO

2. What behaviors tell you that it is or isn't? _____

_____

3. Who is the harasser? _____

4. Who is the victim? _____

5. Who is legally responsible for the harassment? _____

6. What can or should the victim do? Check any that apply:

__ Tell a friend

__ Tell the manager/supervisor

__ Tell a representative from the Human Resources Department

__ Ignore it

__ Follow the workplace sexual harassment policy and procedure

__ File an official complaint (take legal action)

__ Write an informal resolution letter to the harasser

__ Quit the job

__ Get someone else to talk to the harasser

__ Other (describe): _____

_____

_____

CASE STUDY: WORKPLACE #6

Dr. Fran Kelhoffer, Chief of Staff at the local hospital, is attracted to one of the new physicians who just joined the medical staff. She is interested in getting to know him better.

One night after they both finish making their late rounds to visit their patients, Dr. Kelhoffer asks the new doctor if he would like to go out to dinner and a movie the following evening. The new doctor looks stunned, says he has plans to go out of town, and quickly leaves the hospital.

Questions

1. Is this sexual harassment?   YES   NO

2. What behaviors tell you that it is or isn't? _____

_____

3. Who is the harasser? _____

4. Who is the victim? _____

5. Who is legally responsible for the harassment? _____

6. What can or should the victim do? Check any that apply:

__ Tell a friend

__ Tell the manager/supervisor

__ Tell a representative from the Human Resources Department

__ Ignore it

__ Follow the workplace sexual harassment policy and procedure

__ File an official complaint (take legal action)

__ Write an informal resolution letter to the harasser

__ Quit the job

__ Get someone else to talk to the harasser

__ Other (describe): _____

_____

_____

NO LAUGHING MATTER: HIGH SCHOOL STUDENTS & SEXUAL HARASSMENT

by Kathy Moore

The boys don't show
And the girls don't tell
How hard sometimes it is to think
You could ever learn it well.

The girls don't tell
And the boys don't show
How hard sometimes it is to know
You're hurting someone else.

The boys don't show
And the girls don't tell
How hard sometimes it is to think
You could ever learn it well.
Just like a woman
Just like a man
We're all in this together
We all can hurt sometimes.

Doing my work
Feeling able and strong
More to be learned
And it's coming along
Fit it together
Lift it in place
A joke calls me back
To my shape and my face.

Guys that I see
Have so much to lose
Act like a man
There's not much to choose
It's something to prove
You're weak or you're tough
And being yourself
Doesn't seem like enough.

The girls don't tell
And the boys don't show
How hard sometimes it is to know
You're hurting someone else
Trying to think about yourself
You hate to show you care
Want to fit right in somewhere.

The boys don't show
And the girls don't tell
How hard sometimes it is to think
You could ever learn it well.

Just like a woman
Just like a man
We're all in this together
We all can help sometimes.

I'm out in the morning
I swing in the sun
I lift in the breeze
My feet want to run
An ugly laugh
A dirty name
My woman's body
Won't take the blame.

The girls don't tell
And the boys don't show
How hard sometimes it is to know
You're hurting someone else
What are you thinking about yourself
You hate to show you care
Want to fit right in somewhere.

The boys don't show
And the girls don't tell
How hard sometimes it is to think
You could ever learn it well
Just like a woman
Just like a man
We're all in this together
We all can help sometimes.

© Kathy Moore, Solid Ground. Theme song from
*No Laughing Matter: High School Students and
Sexual Harassment* videotape (Massachusetts
Department of Education, May 1982). Written
by Kathy Moore and sung by Solid Ground.
Reprinted by permission of Nan D. Stein, Ed.D.

SEXUAL HARASSMENT SURVEY

Please return your completed survey by _____
                                                              DATE

Your gender is (circle one): MALE   FEMALE   What grade are you in? _____

Please complete the following survey by answering as many questions as you can.
Do not sign your name; your responses will remain anonymous and confidential.
For each question, mark the answer that best describes your thoughts and/or feelings.
For questions with more than one answer, please mark as many as apply.

1. Are you aware of sexual harassment happening in our school...

...between students? __ Yes __ No

...between students and teachers? __ Yes __ No

...between students and other school staff? __ Yes __ No

...between teachers? __ Yes __ No

2. How often do you think sexual harassment happens in our school?

__ All of the time   __ Hardly ever

__ Most of the time   __ Never

__ Some of the time

3. Have you ever sexually harassed another person? __ Yes __ No

4. Have you ever been sexually harassed at school? __ Yes __ No

If "yes," who were the harassers?

__ Student(s)   __ Principal

__ Teacher(s)   __ Janitor/custodian

__ Coach   __ Secretary

__ Other (describe): _____

If you answered "no" to Question 3, skip to Question 18.

5. Read through the list of harassing behaviors on the next page and mark any that have happened to you.

• In the column at the left, write "S" if the harasser was a student, "A" if it was a teacher or other adult staff person.

• In the column at the right, circle "1" if the behavior happened just once, "2" if it happened about once a month, "3" if it happened two to four times a month, "4" if it happened every few days, and "5" if it happened every day.

☞

Student (S) or Adult (A)?	One time	Once/month	2–4 times/month	Every few days	Every day
_____ Staring/looks	1	2	3	4	5
_____ Gestures with hands or body	1	2	3	4	5
_____ Pulling at clothes	1	2	3	4	5
_____ Saying sexual things to me or to others	1	2	3	4	5
_____ Touching/patting/pinching	1	2	3	4	5
_____ Bad vibes/a gut feeling	1	2	3	4	5
_____ Asking to have sex with me	1	2	3	4	5
_____ Cornering/leaning over/following	1	2	3	4	5
_____ Calling me or others sexually offensive names	1	2	3	4	5
_____ Making out (kissing/hugging/touching) in a public place (hallway, gym) where I can see it	1	2	3	4	5
_____ Pressuring me for dates	1	2	3	4	5
_____ Telling dirty jokes or rape jokes	1	2	3	4	5
_____ Rape or attempted rape	1	2	3	4	5
_____ Sexual swear words	1	2	3	4	5
_____ Sexual pictures/cartoons	1	2	3	4	5
_____ Rating my appearance or others' appearance on a scale of 1 to 10	1	2	3	4	5
_____ Comments about my body/weight/clothing, or others' body/weight/clothing	1	2	3	4	5
_____ Being kissed or hugged	1	2	3	4	5
_____ Sexual rumors	1	2	3	4	5
_____ Sexually offensive T-shirts, hats, or pins	1	2	3	4	5
_____ Graffiti	1	2	3	4	5
_____ Winking/licking lips/facial expressions	1	2	3	4	5
_____ Cat calls/whistles	1	2	3	4	5
_____ Kissing sounds/howling	1	2	3	4	5
_____ Sexual notes or letters	1	2	3	4	5
_____ Using computers for sexual games/graffiti/jokes	1	2	3	4	5
Other types of sexual harassment you have seen, heard of, or been a victim of:					
_____ _____	1	2	3	4	5
_____ _____	1	2	3	4	5

☞

6. In general, how long did the harassment continue?

___ 1 week

___ 1 week–2 months

___ 2–6 months

___ 6 months–1 year

___ Longer than a year

7. How did you feel about the harassment?

___ Angry

___ Scared

___ Confused

___ Ashamed

___ I thought I misunderstood the attention

___ Flattered

___ Embarrassed

___ I didn't think it was a big deal

___ I wondered if I did something to cause it

___ I thought that something must be wrong with me

___ I felt that I'm not important

___ I felt the person had a sexist attitude

___ Powerless

___ Guilty

___ Physically sick (stomach ache, headache, etc.). Describe or explain:

_____

___ Other (describe): _____

_____

8. Where did the harassment occur?

___ Classroom

___ Hallway

___ Auditorium

___ Car (on school grounds)

___ Parking lot

___ Teachers' lounge

___ Cafeteria

___ Office (Whose? _____)

___ Gym/locker room

___ Other (describe): _____

_____

9. When did the harassment occur?

___ Before school

___ During class

___ Between classes

___ After school

___ During lunch

___ During a school-sponsored activity (examples: band, athletic event, etc.).

Describe: _____

10. How did you respond to the harassment?

___ Ignored it

___ Went along with it (explain): _____

___ Didn't go to school for a few days

___ Cut the class where the harassment occurred

___ Transferred to another class

___ Quit school

__ Asked/told the person to stop

__ Wrote the person a letter

__ Slapped/hit the person

__ Tried to stay away from the person

__ Threatened to tell on him/her

__ Reported the harasser to:

__ Teacher	__ Police
__ School counselor	__ Lawyer/attorney
__ Principal	__ Human Rights Department
__ Superintendent	__ Department of Education
__ School board member	__ Other (describe):
__ Pastor/priest/rabbi/other clergy member	__ I didn't do any of the things on this list. Instead, I… (describe what you did):
__ Crisis line/hotline	
__ Outside agency (sexual assault center, mental health clinic, etc.)	_____
	_____

11. If you ignored the harassment, what were your reasons?

__ I didn't know what to do

__ I didn't see a need to report it

__ I didn't want to hurt the person's feelings

__ I was too embarrassed

__ I didn't think anything would be done about it

__ I thought I would be blamed for it

__ I didn't think anyone would believe me

__ I was afraid the person would try to get even

__ I didn't want to get the person into trouble

__ Other (describe): _____

_____

12. If you went along with the harassment, what were your reasons?

__ To prevent a lower grade or to get a higher grade

__ I liked the person

__ I needed a job recommendation

__ I needed a recommendation for college/vocational school

__ He/she is popular

__ It made me feel important

__ It made me feel attractive

__ It made me feel loved

__ I thought it would make me more popular

__ I was afraid of what would happen if I didn't go along

__ I didn't want people to think I was weird by not going along

__ I didn't want people to think I couldn't take a joke

__ I wondered if I might be misunderstanding the attention

__ Other (describe): _____

_____

☞

13. If you didn't go along with the harassment, what were your reasons?

__ Fear

__ Anger

__ I knew it was wrong/disrespectful

__ I didn't like the person

__ He/she was too old or too young

__ I was afraid someone would find out

__ I was offended/disgusted/grossed out

__ I didn't think anyone would believe me later

__ I wasn't interested in the person sexually

__ Other (describe): _____

_____

14. Did the harasser say or hint that something bad would happen if you didn't go along? (Examples: loss of friendship, spreading rumors about you, lower grade, etc.)   __ Yes   __ No

If "yes," explain: _____

15. Did the harasser say or hint that something special would happen if you did go along? (Examples: a date, higher grade, job recommendation, popularity, etc.)   __ Yes   __ No

If "yes," explain: _____

16. If you reported the harasser, what effect did this have?

__ It made things better. Explain: _____

__ It made things worse. Explain: _____

__ It didn't have any effect/make any difference

17. Who did you go to for support after the harassment?

__ Nobody

__ Friend

__ Teacher

__ School counselor/dean

__ Boyfriend/girlfriend

__ Parent/guardian

__ Other family member (sister/brother, aunt/uncle, etc.)

__ School administrator

__ Pastor/priest/rabbi/other clergy member

__ Crisis line/hotline

__ Outside agency (sexual assault center, mental health clinic, etc.)

__ Other (describe): _____

_____

18. Is the harasser known for this kind of behavior?   __ Yes   __ No

19. Please add any other thoughts, comments, and ideas you have about sexual harassment in general, sexual harassment in our school, your feelings about sexual harassment, etc. Use the back of the paper if you need more space.

_____

_____

Thank you for completing this survey.

COURSE EVALUATION

Please return your completed survey by _____
DATE

Your gender is (circle one): MALE   FEMALE

What grade are you in? _____

Please answer these questions about SEXUAL HARASSMENT AND TEENS.

1. The course was:

__ too long   __ too short   __ just right

2. The amount of information was:

__ too much   __ too little   __ just right

3. The pace (speed) was:

__ too slow   __ too fast   __ just right

4. For each statement:

Circle 5 if you *strongly agree*

Circle 3 if you *agree*

Circle 1 if you *strongly disagree.*

	Strongly agree	Agree	Strongly disagree
• I learned a lot I didn't know before.	5	3	1
• The course held my interest.	5	3	1
• Things I learned are useful to my life now.	5	3	1
• Things I learned will be useful to my life in the future.	5	3	1
• The course is helping our school now.	5	3	1
• The course will help our school in the future.	5	3	1
• The teacher(s) was prepared.	5	3	1
• I could understand the information being presented.	5	3	1
• The transparencies and handouts were interesting and helpful.	5	3	1
• The activities were interesting and helpful.	5	3	1

☞

5. Complete these sentences:

- The most helpful activity was _____

- The most important activity was _____

- The most eye-opening activity was _____

- My least favorite activity was _____

   Why was this your least favorite activity? _____

   _____

6. Have your beliefs about male and female roles, relationships, etc. changed because of this course? __ YES __ NO

   Please explain: _____

   _____

7. What improvements would you make to this course?

   _____

   _____

8. What would you like your school to do next about sexual harassment? Check as many as apply:

   __ Offer support groups for victims

   __ Offer groups for harassers to make them more aware of how their behavior affects other people

   __ Require all students, teachers, staff, and parents to learn about sexual harassment

   __ Make sure victims know about community resources that can help them

9. Would you recommend this course to someone else? __ YES __ NO

   Explain: _____

   _____

10. Give an example of something you plan to change in your own life as a result of this course.

   _____

   _____

11. Give this course a final grade from 1 to 5, with 5 being the highest grade. Circle one:

   5   4   3   2   1

Thank you for completing this evaluation.

ADDITIONAL READINGS AND RESOURCES

READINGS

Sex Equity Handbook for Schools. New York: Longman, 1982.

Tune In To Your Rights: A Guide for Teen-agers About Turning Off Sexual Harassment. Ann Arbor: Center for Sex Equity in Schools, University of Michigan, 1985.

Adams, Caren, et al. *No Is Not Enough: Helping Teen-agers Avoid Sexual Assault.* San Luis Obispo, CA: Impact Publishers, 1984.

Backhouse, Connie. *Fighting Sexual Harassment: An Advocacy Handbook.* Cambridge: Alliance Against Sexual Coercion, 1981.

Bell, Ruth, ed. *Changing Bodies Changing Lives.* New York: Random House, 1980.

Benson, Donna and Gregg Thomson. *Sex, Gender and Power: Sexual Harassment on a University Campus.* Berkeley: University of California, 1979.

Center for Sex Equity in Schools. "Sexual Harassment Is No Laughing Matter." *Title IX Line:* Special Issue (Fall 1983). Ann Arbor: University of Michigan School of Education.

Clarke, Elissa. *Stopping Sexual Harassment.* Detroit: Labor Education and Research Project, 1980.

de Nys, Mary, and Leslie R. Wolfe. "Learning Her Place: Sex Bias in the Elementary School Classroom." *Peer Report 5* (Autumn 1985).

Field, Anne. "Harassment on Campus: Sex In a Tenured Position?" *MS.* (September 1989): 68–73, 100–102.

Flerchinger, Billie Jo and Jennifer J. Fay. *Top Secret.* Santa Cruz: Network Publication, King County Rape Relief, 1982.
— *Top Secret: A Discussion Guide.* Santa Cruz: Network Publication, King County Rape Relief, 1985.

Gilligan, Carol. *In A Different Voice.* Cambridge: Harvard University Press, 1982.

Griffin, Thomas M. "Sexual Harassment and Title IX." *West's Education Law Reporter 18* (1984): 513–520.

Hall, Roberta, and Bernice Sandler. "The Classroom Climate: A Chilly One for Women?" Paper written for the Project on the Status and Education of Women, Association of American Colleges, 1982.

Harragan, B.L. "Sexual Harassment—Put Out or Get Out." In *Games Mother Never Taught You: Corporate Gamesmanship for Women.* New York: Warner Communications Company, 1979.

Kaser, Joyce and Marlene Ross. "Preventing Sexual Harassment of School Employees." *Educational Leadership* (November 1983): 53–57.

Mead, Margaret. "A Proposal: We Need Taboos on Sex at Work." *Redbook* (April 1978): 31, 33, 38.

National Advisory Council on Women's Educational Programs. *A Report on the Sexual Harassment of Students.* Washington, DC: NACWEP, U.S. Department of Education, 1980.

Powell, Elizabeth. *Talking Back to Sexual Pressure.* Minneapolis: CompCare Publishers, 1991.

Project on the Status and Education of Women. *Sexual Harassment: A Hidden Issue.* Washington, DC: Association of American Colleges, 1978.

Riley, Susan. *A Fair Shot/An Equal Chance.* Quincy: Project SCOPE, Massachusetts Department of Education, 1980.

Rossein, Merrick. "Sex Discrimination and the Sexually Charged Work Environment." *The New York University Review of Law and Social Change 9* (Fall 1981): 271–305.

Rowe, Mary P. "Ideas for Action: Dealing with Sexual Harassment." *Harvard Business Review* 59:3 (May–June 1981): 42–46.

Sadker, Myra, and David Sadker. "Sexism in the Classroom." *Vocational Education Journal* (October 1985): 30–32.

Safran, Claire. "What Men Do to Women on the Job: A Shocking Look at Sexual Harassment." *Redbook* (November 1976): 149, 217–223.

Shakeshaft, Carol. "A Gender At Risk." *Phi Delta Kappan* (March 1986): 499–503.

Stein, Nan D., Ed.D. "It Happens Here Too: Sexual Harassment in the Schools." *Education Week* (November 17, 1991): 32, 25.

Strauss, Susan. *Sexual Harassment to Teenagers: It's Not Fun/It's Illegal.* St. Paul: Minnesota Department of Education, Equal Educational Opportunities Section, 1987.

Stringer, Gayle M. and Deanna Rants-Rodriguez. *So What's It to Me? Sexual Assault Information for Boys.* Renton, WA: King County Rape Relief, 1987.

Till, F. J. *Sexual Harassment: A Report On the Sexual Harassment of Students.* Washington, DC: National Advisory Council on Women's Educational Programs, 1980.

Toufexis, Anastasia. "Our Violent Kids." *Time* (June 12, 1989): 52–58.

Vandell, Kathy and Lauren Fishbein. "Equitable Treatment of Girls and Boys in the Classroom," a brief prepared for the American Association of University Women, 1989.

RESOURCES

Dreamworlds: Desire/Sex/Power in Rock Video. A powerful one-hour video depicting images from a variety of music videos. The accompanying narration describes the patterns in the images and how they contribute to attitudes about women as easy prey for sexual assault.

> Project of the Center for the Study of Communication
> University of Massachusetts at Amherst
> Foundation for Media Education
> PO Box 2008
> Amherst, MA 01004-2002
> (413) 545-2341

Handling the Sexual Harassment Complaint. A how-to video dealing with the various aspects of handling a sexual harassment complaint in your organization.

> American Media Incorporated
> 1454 30th Street
> West Des Moines, IA 50265-1390
> 1-800-262-2557

Killing Us Softly. A half-hour video or film depicting media images of women.

> Cambridge Documentary Films
> P.O. Box 385
> Cambridge, MA 02139
> (617) 354-3677

No Laughing Matter: High School Students and Sexual Harassment. A 25-minute VHS videotape which presents the stories of three high school teens who are involved in incidents of sexual harassment at school and work. Comments by teachers and administrators regarding the prevention of sexual harassment are interspersed with the stories.

> Massachusetts Department of Education
> 1385 Hancock Street
> Quincy, MA 02169
> (617) 770-7508

Power Pinch: Sexual Harassment in the Workplace. A half-hour film which focuses on sexual harassment in the workplace; includes interviews with victims, vignettes, legal explanations, and excerpts from a staff training workshop.

> Coronet/MTI Film and Video
> 108 Wilmot Road
> Deerfield, IL 60015
> (800) 323-5431

Sexual Harassment in the Workplace...Identify. Stop. Prevent. A 23-minute video dealing with the definition of sexual harassment and suggestions for preventing it from occurring, stopping it if it does occur, and identifying types of sexual harassment. Includes training leader's guide and desk reminder cards.

> American Media Incorporated
> 1454 30th Street
> West Des Moines, Iowa 50265-1390
> 1-800-262-2557

Sexual Harassment: It's Uncool. A dramatic poster to spark discussion. Includes a definition of sexual harassment and reporting information.

> Project Esteem
> The Hawaii Department of Education
> 1390 Miller Street, Suite 416
> Honolulu, HI 96813

Sexual Harassment on the Job. A half-hour video excerpt from the Phil Donahue Show.

> Films for the Humanities
> P.O. Box 2053
> Princeton, NJ 08543
> (609) 452-1128

Sexual Harassment: Walking the Corporate Fine Line. A 21-minute video which traces the legal history of sexual harassment, points out the damage sexual harassment can do to the organization and the individual, and spells out what the policy should contain.

> NOW Legal Defense and Education Fund
> 99 Hudson Street
> New York, NY 10013
> (212) 925-6635

Touch (video for grades K–6) and *No Easy Answers* (curriculum and video for grades 6–12) deal with sexual abuse prevention. The half-hour videos can be used alone or to supplement existing abuse prevention programs in schools, churches, and community groups.

> Illusion Theatre
> 528 Hennepin Avenue, Suite 704
> Minneapolis, MN 55403
> (612) 339-4944

INDEX

U

United States Army, sexual harassment of women in, 11

United States Department of Education, 5

University of Massachusetts at Amherst, 142

V

Verbal harassment, 3

Verbal sexual conduct, defined, 43, 60

Victims

blaming, 13, 75, 98

both genders as, 47

defined, 60

effects on, 97-98

female, 9

lack of reporting by, 13, 71, 77, 102, 117

male, 9

in nontraditional jobs, 11, 76

perceptions of, 46

in schools, 7

and self-blame, 13, 98

services for, 31

and stages of grieving, 13

understanding and supporting, 12-15

Videos, as resources, 2, 142

Violence, in media, 19. *See also* Sexual violence

Vulnerability

decreasing, 7

of special needs students, 8

W

Warshaw, Robin, 13, 19

Who's Hurt and Who's Liable: Sexual Harassment in Massachusetts Schools, 19, 133

Women

of color as victims, 77

earning power of, 66

exploited by advertising, 67, 68

in nontraditional jobs, 11, 76

as property, 65

status of, 65

as target of sexual harassment, 2

See also Girls; Teenage females

Working Woman magazine, 12

Workplace

case studies, 104, 109-111, 127-132

effects of harassment in, 14, 98

exploited in advertising, 67

legal liability of, 77

professional women in, 75

reporting of sexual harassment incidents in, 71

sexual harassment in, 3, 4, 7, 10-12, 49-50, 70, 72, 75, 98, 104, 115

and women in nontraditional jobs, 11, 76

Susan Strauss is a Senior Training and Organization Development Specialist at Abbott Northwestern Hospital in Minneapolis, Minnesota. An active leader in sexual harassment programs and policies, she has designed and directed educational training programs on sexual harassment throughout Minnesota, and she has assisted in the development of sexual harassment policies for school districts within the state. Ms. Strauss has assisted the Minnesota Attorney General's office in passing two bills concerning sexual harassment and sexual violence in secondary and post-secondary institutions. She does sexual harassment consulting and training on sexual harassment to schools, organizations, and the Minnesota Department of Education, Sex Equity Division.

Ms. Strauss is also the author of "Sexual Harassment in the School: Legal Implications for Principals" *(NASSP Bulletin)*, and a curriculum distributed to Minnesota schools upon which this book is based.

Pamela Espeland is author of 8 books, coauthor of 6 books, and editor of over 100 books of nonfiction for educators, parents, and children including *The Kid's Guide to Social Action* by Barbara A. Lewis (Free Spirit Publishing, 1991), *Stick Up For Yourself! Every Kid's Guide to Personal Power and Positive Self-Esteem* by Gershen Kaufman and Lev Raphael (Free Spirit Publishing, 1990), *Evaluating and Treating Adult Children of Alcoholics* by Timmen Cermak, M.D. (Johnson Institute, 1991), and *Women's Reality* by Anne Wilson Schaef (Winston Press, 1980). She has been Editor in Chief for Free Spirit Publishing since 1985.